Shading Flowers

The Complete Guide for Rug Hookers

Jeanne Field

STACKPOLE
BOOKS

Copyright © 1991 by Stackpole Books

Published by
STACKPOLE BOOKS
Cameron and Kelker Streets
P.O. Box 1831
Harrisburg, PA 17105

Printed in the United States of America

First Edition

10 9 8 7 6 5 4 3

Library of Congress Cataloging-in-Publication Data

Field, Jeanne.
    Shading flowers : the complete guide for rug hookers / Jeanne
Field. — 1st ed.
        p.   cm.
    ISBN 0-8117-3081-6 : $16.95
    1. Hooking. 2. Flowers in art. I. Title.
TT833.F54   1991
746.7'4—dc20   91-13129
                                                    CIP

For Lloyd, who has never held a hook in his hand—what patience and support!

Contents

The Flowers

Anemone

Aster

Buttercup

Calla Lily

Camelia

Canterbury Bells

Chinese Lantern

Chrysanthemum

Columbine

Cosmos

Crocus

Daffodil

Daisy

Dogwood

Foxglove

Geranium

Hepatica

Hibiscus

Holly

Hollyhock

Iris

Jack-in-the-Pulpit

Lilac

Lily of the Valley

Lupin

Magnolia

Morning Glory

Nasturtium

Orchid

Pansy

Peony

Petunia

Poinsettia

Poppy

Primrose

Pussy Willow

Queen Anne's Lace

Roses

Rose Buds

Silver Dollar

Sweet Pea

Tiger Lily

Trillium

Tulips

Violet

Introduction

Although there are many beautiful floral designs available, some rug hookers hesitate to attempt such projects because they don't know how to shade flowers. This book provides an introduction to the art of shading flowers; and the use of numbered and shaded illustrations makes it easy to understand. The book will take you step-by-step through the shading of forty-five flowers and will guide you in improving your technique.

The flowers you find in your rug design may be shaped or positioned differently from the examples that have been provided, nevertheless the basic techniques presented can be adapted to the flowers found in any floral rug design.

If you have never been exposed to gardening and nursery catalogs, you may be unaware of the names, shapes, and sizes of annual and perennial garden flowers. My students often ask me to point out and name specific flowers that are found in their designs. Since this book may introduce you to some flowers that you don't recognize, I have included brief notes about the origin and characteristics of each flower, as well as the directions for shading it.

Basics of Rug Hooking

Hooking rugs is by no means a new craft. It began many years ago on the northeastern seaboard of North America in Acadia and New England. Today the technique of rug hooking is much the same as it has always been. We still use a hook and a printed or hand-drawn design on a chosen backing. We still love the "primitive mat," but over the years, we have also developed a refined technique for making fine floral rugs and wall hangings.

Equipment Needed

A hook. The hook used in rug hooking is a crochet hook set in a wooden handle. Hooks are available in different sizes, depending on the width of the wool strips being used.

A foundation for the design. The foundation can be an even-weave, 14-ounce burlap or a linen or cotton that has a 10 to 14 vertical and horizontal thread count.

A hoop or frame. A wooden hoop is the least expensive. It should be 14 inches in diameter.

Scissors. Scissors need a good point and should be sharp.

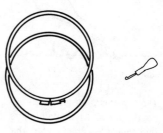

The hoop and hook have long been the basic equipment for rug hookers.

Fabric. The fabric of choice for rug hooking is an even-weave wool flannel. It should be 100 percent wool, a 12-ounce weight. Wool has great durability and it forms a soft loop. Synthetic fabrics tend to be stiff and often shred.

Preparation of Fabric

All fabric, new and recycled, should be washed before it is cut into strips. The wool can be cut by hand into 1/4-inch strips. Just make sure the wool is cut on the straight grain of the fabric. You can just nick the fabric with scissors and then rip it. Or you can use a cutting machine, which will cut the wool in even strips. (The machine uses interchangeable cutting wheels to cut different widths of strips.)

Technique of Basic Hooking

Now that you know what you need and how to prepare the fabric, you're ready to begin hooking! Find a comfortable chair, relax, and enjoy learning the technique of basic hooking.

Put the burlap pattern right side up in your hoop. Use the thumb screw to tighten the pattern and to keep it taut. As you hook, the hoop can rest on your knee or on the edge of a table.

Hold the hook comfortably in the palm of your writing hand with the barb of the hook up. Hold the strip of wool between the thumb and index finger of your other hand. As you hold the wool strip, keep your hand under the pattern, up against the burlap.

Insert the hook through the burlap, catching the whole width of the strip and bringing the end through the burlap to the top side. The end should be approximately 1/2 inch to 1 inch in height.

Skip 1, 2, or 3 holes in the burlap (depending on the width of the strip of fabric), and insert the hook again, bringing up a loop of the wool strip through this hole to a height of 1/4 inch. Continue pulling up loops until you come to the end of the wool strip. Then bring the end of the wool to the top side of your work. (The ends can be cut off even with the loops when you have completed a small area of hooking.) To continue hooking, pull another wool strip through the same hole as the strip that was just finished and repeat the procedure.

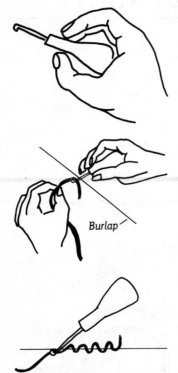

Burlap

The proper grip on the hook— handle in palm, barb pointing up—should feel comfortable. The hook is used to pull the wool strip through the burlap into loops 1/4 inch high.

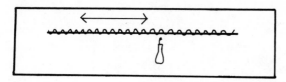

The hook should be held perpendicular to the direction in which you are hooking.

Note: There should be no burlap showing between the loops, but don't try to pull a loop up in every hole of the burlap. The loops should just touch one another—without bunching up.

The best way to achieve the proper technique is to practice. Try the exercises below, holding the hook so that it is perpendicular to the direction in which you are hooking.

Hook several straight rows—some horizontal, some vertical, some going to the right, some going to the left, some going up, and some going down. Hook several wavy lines.

Hook several rows close together to form a pile.

At first, your loops will be uneven, but keep on practicing until you can pull the loops up easily and can keep them at the same height.

When you have hooked a few rows, turn your work over and check the back. It should be flat and smooth. You should never carry a strip of wool across an area that you have already hooked. When you reach a place where you can go no further, cut your wool and start again where there is no hooking in the way.

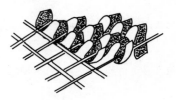

With a little practice, you will be able to keep all your loops at the same height.

Techniques in Shading

Before discussing the techniques of shading flowers, it might be helpful to review the parts of a flower. Flowers usually have a ring of showy *petals*. Sometimes the petals are fused into a tube or funnel. Below the petals are the *sepals*; the sepals look like little leaves that form a cup, or *calyx*, that holds the petals. The sepals are usually green, but once in a while they are the same color as the petals. In the center of the flower, the *stamen* includes *anthers*, the parts that usually bear the pollen, and the stalks that support them. Stamens vary in number and arrangement in different kinds of flowers. When you are directed to hook the center of a flower first, it means you should begin with the stamen.

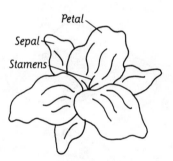

When hooking, you should give individual attention to each part of the flower.

Shapes of Flowers

For the purpose of shading flowers, we can classify them by their shapes. This will help make the study of how to shade flowers easy and understandable.

We will consider seven flower shapes:

1. Open-petaled flowers with large petals
2. Open-petaled flowers with small petals

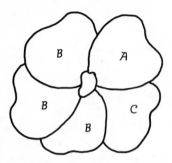

A petals are completely visible; B petals are obscured on one side; C petals are obscured on both sides. Observing these distinctions while hooking will create an illusion of depth in your rug.

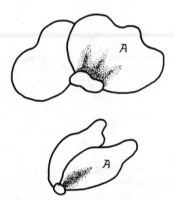

As the top or nearest petals, the A petals contain the lightest values. The center base is the darkest part of the A petal—ranging from value 6 for large petals to value 3 for small ones—and it shades to value 1 at the petal's tip.

3. Many-petaled flowers with narrow petals
4. Large bell-shaped flowers
5. Small bell-shaped flowers
6. Funnel- or tube-shaped flowers
7. Irregular flowers

Positions of the Petals

In order to make a shaded flower appear three dimensional, each petal is placed in one of three positions. By shading the petals according to their positions, you can create an illusion of depth.

A Petals. These petals are complete petals; no other petals overlap them or hide parts of them. These petals are in front of, or on top of, other petals. They will be the lightest in value.

B Petals. These petals are half complete because they are partly obscured on one side by other petals. They will be hooked in the medium values.

C Petals. These petals are incomplete because they are obscured on both sides by other petals; they appear to be under other petals. These petals will be the darkest value.

Shading the Petals

By noting the positions of the petals, you can shade them from dark to light to give a three-dimensional effect with shadows and highlights. You can accomplish this by hooking with shades of a color that range from dark to light.

As you read the directions for shading flowers, you will see references to the *center base*. The center base is where the base of the petal meets the center of the flower. You will use a dark value at the center base. You will also use a dark value to indicate a shadow where one petal goes under another; the area along the edge of the petal where it is partly covered by another petal will be shaded.

A Petals. We know that these petals appear to be on top of the others and that they will be the lightest values. All A petals will be dark at the center base, becoming lighter at the tips and outer edges of the petals. A small petal could be shaded from a dark color of value 3 to value 1. A large petal could be shaded from a dark color of value 6 to value 1.

B Petals. A B petal is visible on one side, but it goes under another petal on the other side. All B petals will be dark at the center base and dark along the edge where one petal goes under another. Depending on the size of the petal, you could choose a dark color of value 4, 5, or 6.

C Petals. A C petal is only visible at the center and upper portion of the petal; it is obscured on both sides by other petals. All C petals will be dark at the center base and dark along the edges where one petal goes under another. The dark color chosen, probably value 6, will be hooked from one side of the petal where it goes under another petal to the other side where it goes under another petal. A much darker petal will result, probably not requiring the lighter values.

Before you start hooking a flower, you should examine it to determine what position each petal holds; identify the A, B, and C petals. Then use the information given above as a guide to hooking each flower.

The Order of Hooking

If you carefully follow the order of hooking provided below, the shading of a flower will fall into place without difficulty.

1. Hook the centers.
2. Hook the rolls and turnunders on petals.
3. Hook all A petals.
4. Hook all B petals.
5. Hook all C petals.

You will find that some flowers won't have a center and some won't have any turnunders, but most flowers will have varied numbers of A, B, and C petals.

Not only do we hook each flower in a specific order, but we do the same thing with a grouping of flowers, such as violets. Hook the flowers that are on top first; then work your way to the flowers underneath.

To guide you in the correct order of hooking the parts of a flower, two illustrations are provided with the directions for each flower. The first illustration is a numbered drawing in which 1 indicates the lightest value and 6 indicates the darkest. The location of the numbers shows the area that each color should cover; the numbers do not indicate how many

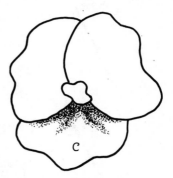

The B petal is darkest—use values of 4, 5, or 6—at the center base and where it seems to disappear under another petal.

The C petal is darkest at the center base and where it seems to disappear under other petals. These areas should be hooked with a dark value 6 and shaded with medium values.

rows or loops to hook, since that will vary with the size of the pattern. The positions of the A, B, and C petals are indicated outside the numbered illustration.

The second illustration is a shaded drawing that will show you where the shadows and highlights are located on each flower. Outside the shaded illustration, there are numbers that give the order in which the parts of the flower should be hooked. You should follow the suggested sequence carefully. Try to use both illustrations when you hook a flower.

Note: Some flowers, such as tube-shaped, funnel-shaped, or bell-shaped flowers, don't have petals. The directions for hooking these flowers will include specific suggestions for the order of hooking them.

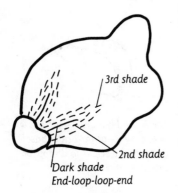

The darkest fingers should be hooked with an end-loop-loop-end and followed with progressively lighter shades.

The Selection of Color

Choosing color is a very personal aspect of hooking a rug. To help you decide on a color scheme, browse through flower books, seed catalogs, and home decorating magazines. Look at the color schemes you have in your home—the draperies, wallpapers, fabrics, and floor coverings that you have already chosen.

First consider a color for the background of your rug. The background determines the color of the rug; if the background is green, the rug will be considered a green rug. Keep in mind that the flower colors will stand out better against a light or a dark background than they will against a medium-colored background.

By hooking up one side, ending, and then hooking down the other side, you can create fingers with sharp points.

To test a range of possible flower colors, lay swatches of color on the background color you have chosen. Work with the colors until you have a handsome combination. Remember that there should be a contrast between the edge of the flowers and the background. If the background is dark, the edges of the flowers should be medium or light. If the background is light, the edges of the flowers should be medium.

As you choose the colors for a floral rug, you may want to consider one of the following kinds of color schemes.

Realistic. In a realistic color scheme, the colors of flowers are just as they are in a garden: there are red roses, yellow daisies, purple pansies, and blue morning glories. Avoid bright, brash colors. Choose slightly grayed colors for a pleasing combination.

Monochromatic. In a monochromatic color scheme, different values and intensities of a single color are used for all of the flowers. The only other colors in the rug would be found in the leaves and the background.

Decorator. A decorator color scheme is built by choosing the colors from a wallpaper or fabric. The colors may not be realistic, but they have designer influence and they can make a very appealing choice.

The Shading Techniques

Fingering. To make a smooth and realistic transition from one shade to the next, we hook the shading in "fingers." Throughout the book, you will see references to an *end-loop-end* or an *end-loop-loop-end* to indicate the number of loops required to cover a specific area, depending on how far the strip of fabric must go.

It is helpful to end the strip at the top of the finger and start again just below it on the other side. It takes practice to make pointed fingers, but learning to make them will add much to your shading. As you become familiar with fingering, you will eventually be able to go up one side of the finger, turn, and come down the other side, making a good point at the top of the finger.

Do not let the fingers become rounded.

You may have more than one finger of shading on a petal, depending on the size of the petal. Use an end-loop-loop-end for the first fingers on the petal, except when you are working with long petals. The fingers fan out from the center base of the petal. If the space between the fingers becomes too large, another finger can be added in the same shade you are using.

The fingers may not always be the same length on a petal.

Try to make the fingers curved, following the contour of the petal. You don't want them to look like sticks.

When you are hooking a large petal with six values of a color, you will need to repeat one or all of the values in order to have an even shading throughout the petal. Values can be repeated as many times as needed, but they must be hooked in

Rounded fingers—created by hooking lazily around the finger— add little to your rug.

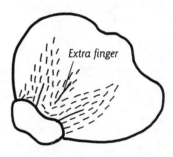

If the space between fingers appears too large, hook in another in the same shade.

A petal's fingers should be of varying lengths, but each should point toward the tip of the petal.

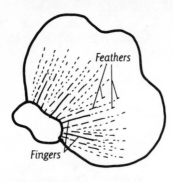

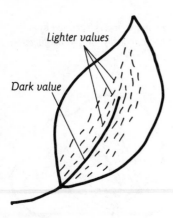

Feathers extend down into the space between the first set of fingers and follow the contour of the petal.

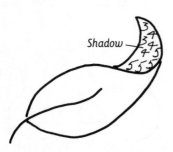

A mock-shaded leaf is shaded from side to side with gentle curves.

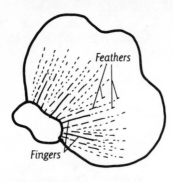

A turnunder must be shadowed—hooked in darker values—to contrast with the rest of the petal.

order. For example, you might hook value 6, then value 5, then value 4. If, at that point, you found that you still had a long way to go to finish the petal, you could repeat value 4. You might also decide to repeat value 3, then hook value 2 and value 1.

Feathering. Feathering is another type of shading that gives the same effect as fingering. It enables you to change values without forming a band of color.

To feather, begin by hooking the fingers needed for the petal, depending on its size. Use an end-loop-loop-end or an end-loop-loop-loop-end, again depending on the size of the petal. Once the beginning fingers are hooked, start feathering about two loops beyond the first fingers. Hook into the spaces between the fingers to the base of the petal.

You should change values with each new set of feathers. Remember that a large petal will require repetition of some or all of the values. Keep your hooking lines curved toward the edge of the petal, and continue feathering to the edge. I really like this type of shading, but it takes practice, so don't be discouraged after a single try.

Mock Shading. As its name implies, this type of shading is an imitation of real shading. The petal or leaf is shaded from side to side. On narrow leaves, a dark value would be hooked two-thirds up one edge of the leaf. Then the other values would be added, each value extending at least two loops beyond the previous one. On wider leaves, half of the leaf would be hooked and then the other half would be hooked.

Examine the example carefully. As you hook a floral rug, you will want to hook some of the leaves with mock shading to add a nice variety to the overall appearance.

Turnunders. Petals often have a flip at the end—a turnunder—to add a little character to the flower. Turnunders are shadowed where they go under the main part of the petal. They may be hooked in values 5, 4, and 3, or in values 3, 2, and 1. There must be a good contrast at the turn.

Rolls. Some petals form a roll on the edge. For example, a rose may have as many as four rolls on its petals. Hook the rolls in light values; hook small rolls in value 1 and larger rolls in values 3 and 1, or 2 and 1.

Ruffled or Fluted Petals. Many larger petals are ruffled or fluted along the edges. Ruffles add a great deal to the shading of a flower, but I usually don't even mention them to beginners. However, once you become accustomed to shading, you will find this type of refinement easy.

To hook a ruffled petal, hook a shadow on the inner curve of the ruffle or fluted edge. The shadow must be two values darker than the surrounding value. Hook three-fourths of the petal, hook the shadow at the edge, and then continue hooking the petal up to the shadow.

Creases. Creases occur near the tips of petals. (Note the illustration of the tiger lily.) The crease line forms a light side and a shadow side. The shadow side must be two values darker than the light side. If the light side is value 1, the shadow side will be value 3.

Bulges. As you shade flowers or leaves, you should try to keep a nice curve to the rows of hooking. But if you see straight lines appearing once in a while, hook an end-loop-end or an end-loop-loop-end where a curve is needed. Hook the end-loop-end with the shade you were using. When you hook the next shade, the bulge will cause you to hook around it, giving a curve to your hooking. You can do this once or several times.

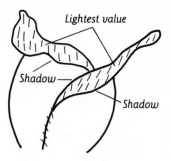

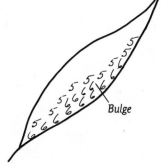

A roll occurs on the edge of a petal. It should be hooked in a lighter value than the rest of the petal. Larger rolls will have a shadow on their outer edge.

A ruffled petal has a shadow along an inner curve. Hook this shadow two values darker than the surrounding values.

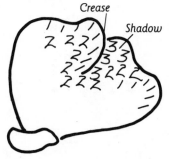

A crease marks a contrast in a petal. The bottom side of the crease should be two values darker than the top.

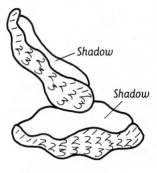

A bulge—hooked with a single end-loop-end or end-loop-loop-end—creates a smooth, natural curve.

Dyeing Swatches

As you become deeply involved in the craft of rug hooking, you may find it desirable—or necessary—to enhance your rug by dyeing your own wool. For those of you who would like to dye your own swatches, I have included methods and formulas for dyeing wool for floral rugs. This chapter will explain the technique of open-pan dyeing of swatches.

The swatches can be conveniently dyed in your kitchen using your range, and happily enough, with very little mess. Follow the instructions carefully. It is not wise to hurry or to cut corners; this will only result in flawing your masterpiece. You should record accurately just what you have done to dye a swatch, so that if you need to dye more wool an exact color, you will have a good chance of duplicating the desired shade.

Definition of Terms

Swatch. Wool that is dyed several values of color ranging from dark to light. Swatches can be made of six, seven, or eight pieces of wool. The swatches discussed here have six values.

Value. The relative lightness or darkness of a color.

Hue. A true color, such as red, green, or blue.

Chroma. The intensity of a color, its brightness or dullness.

Straight Gradation. Dyeing a swatch from a light shade of a color to a darker shade of the same color. (In this book, the dye formula used to produce a straight gradation is referred to as the A *formula.*)

Transitional Swatch. Dyeing a swatch from a light shade of one color to a dark shade of another color. (The dye formula used to produce a transitional swatch is referred to as the B *formula.*)

Dye Bath. This is the heated water to which you will add your dye and wool.

Dye Formula. The dye formula is the solution obtained by mixing dry dye with boiling water in a 1- or 2-cup measuring cup. You will take the amount of dye needed for each value from this solution.

Formula Measurements. This is the amount of dye formula that will be added to the dye bath for each value.

Equipment Needed

Dyes. Cushing dyes are used in all the formulas presented in this book.

Wool flannel. Use white or off-white wool in 9-by-12-inch pieces.

Two enamel or stainless steel pans. These should be 2-quart pans.

Tongs.

Several large stirring spoons.

Glass measuring cups. It's helpful to have 1-cup and 2-cup measuring cups.

Dye spoons. Triple Over Dye (TOD) measuring spoons have been used with great success. These spoons measure $1/4$ teaspoon at one end and $1/32$ teaspoon at the other end.

Set of aluminum measuring spoons.

White vinegar. The vinegar acts as an agent to set the color.

Rubber gloves.

Electric kettle.

Basin for soaking wool.

Paper towels and newspaper to protect table surfaces.

Preparation of Wool

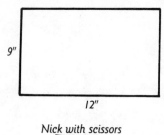

Use white or off-white wool flannel that has a close weave. Each A formula (the dye formula that produces a straight gradation) will dye four six-value swatches. For each B formula (the dye formula that produces a transitional gradation), use two A-dyed swatches, or half of the A-dyed wool.

The size of each piece of wool to be dyed should be 9 inches long by 12 inches wide. Fold the wool in half and then in half again; then nick it with a pair of scissors. Do not rip the wool. Cut six pieces of wool in this manner.

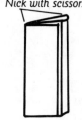

Nick with scissors

Dye each piece of wool separately. The first piece will be the lightest and the last piece will be the darkest. Dye each set of six pieces with the A formula of your choice. The gradation of the swatch should produce a smooth transition from light to dark.

The wool for swatches should be folded in half twice and then nicked at the edge of each fold.

Method of Dyeing

1. Soak the wool in water to which you have added a small amount of dish detergent. Let the wool soak overnight or for at least four hours.

2. Fill two pans three-quarters full of hot water. Bring the water to a boil, and then reduce heat to allow the water to simmer. This is the dye bath.

3. Select the dyes for the specific formula you want to use. Measure the correct amount of dry dye into a 1-cup measuring cup. Add boiling water to the 1-cup level and stir the mixture well. This is the dye formula.

4. *Value 1.* Stir 1 teaspoon of dye formula into the dye bath. Add a 9-by-12-inch piece of wool, and stir the wool to allow the dye to be evenly absorbed. Add 1 tablespoon of vinegar, stirring well. When the water is clear, remove the wool to a sink, rinse it, and squeeze out the excess moisture. Lay the strip of wool nearby so that you will have it for comparison when other shades are dyed.

5. *Value 2.* Stir 2 teaspoons of dye formula into the dye bath. Add a 9-by-12-inch piece of wool, and stir. Add 1 tablespoon of

vinegar, and stir. When the water is clear, remove the wool, rinse it, and squeeze it. Lay the piece of wool next to the dyed value 1 for comparison.

6. *Values 3 to 6.* Dye each of the remaining pieces of wool in the same manner. The formula measurements—the amount of dye formula added to the dye bath for each value—are as follows:

Value 1 = 1 teaspoon
Value 2 = 2 teaspoons
Value 3 = 1 tablespoon
Value 4 = 2 tablespoons
Value 5 = 4 tablespoons
Value 6 = 8 tablespoons

You may find that when you dye the deeper values, the water in the pan will not become clear; it will have a certain murkiness. To decide when to remove the wool from the pan, you will need to keep looking at the pieces that have already been dyed to confirm that there is an even gradation of color. If you want to check a piece of wool, remove it from the dye bath, rinse it, and squeeze out excess water. (The wool will appear darker when it is wet.) Then compare it with the previously dyed values. If the value is correct, leave it with the other dyed material. If it is not dark enough, put it back into the dye bath to absorb more color. It may take a longer simmering time to obtain the darker values. You may even need to add a little more dye.

7. When all six values have been dyed, add ¼ cup of vinegar to the second pan of simmering water, and place all the wool in the pan. After the wool has simmered for 15 minutes, remove it from the pan, rinse it, and dry it. You can dry the wool in a clothes dryer without damaging the fabric.

Variations of Dyeing

You will often need a transitional swatch when hooking floral rugs. A transitional swatch has values ranging from the dark shade of one color to the light shade of another color. It is obtained by using the B formula. To dye a transitional swatch, start with half of the previously dyed material in its six values.

Since the A formula and the B formula go so well together, it is easy to dye the B section when the straight gradation is dyed. You won't even need to dry the dyed material; simply rip the swatch in half and proceed.

You need to use only one pan. Fill the pan two-thirds full of hot water. Bring the water to a boil, and then reduce the heat to allow the water to simmer. Measure the correct amount of dry dye directly into the simmering water, stirring well. Then add 2 tablespoons of vinegar. Place the pieces of wool to be overdyed in the pan. In some B formulas, these pieces will be the three light values; in others, the pieces will be the three darker values. Some formulas require overdyeing all six values. After the wool has simmered for 10 minutes, remove it from the water, rinse it, and dry it. Before drying all the wool, it is a good idea to pin the A-dyed pieces together, separately from the B-dyed pieces. Then the dried swatches can be ripped once again, producing four swatches from each original A swatch: two from formula A and two from formula B.

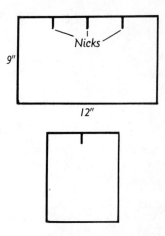

A transitional swatch—with values ranging from a dark shade of one color to a light shade of another color—is created by ripping in half (at the center nick) a swatch dyed with the A formula.

Dye Formulas

Blues.

A. *A lovely gray-blue.*
   Silver-Gray: 1/8 tsp. + 1/16 tsp.
   Blue: 1/16 tsp. + 1/32 tsp.
B. *The same gray-blue going to pink.*
   Dye values 1, 2, and 3 in Old Rose: 1/32 tsp.

A. *A rich dark blue.*
   Navy: 1/4 tsp.
B. *The same blue with a soft mauve overtone.*
   Dye all values in Plum: 1/32 tsp.

Purples.

A. *A pansy purple.*
   Purple: 1/4 tsp.
   Blue: 1/32 tsp.
B. *The same purple going to gray-blue.*
   Dye values 1, 2, and 3 in Blue: 1/32 tsp.

A. *A soft lavender.*
   Lavender: $1/4$ tsp.
B. *The same lavender going to blue.*
   Dye values 1, 2, and 3 in Blue: $1/128$ tsp. (the amount of dye on the end of a toothpick)

Reds.

A. *A vibrant red-orange.*
   Crimson: $1/4$ tsp.
B. *The same red, gently subdued.*
   Dye all values in Wild Rose: $1/32$.

A. *A soft red-orange.*
   Turkey Red: $1/4$ tsp.
   Cardinal: $1/32$ tsp.
   Buttercup Yellow: $1/32$ tsp.
B. *The same red-orange with darker values.*
   Dye values 4, 5, and 6 in Green: $1/128$ tsp.

A. *A mahogany red.*
   Mahogany: $1/4$ tsp.
   Terra Cotta: $1/32$ tsp.
B. *A rich red mahogany.*
   Dye values 1, 2, and 3 in Cardinal: $1/32$ tsp.

A. *A pastel pink.*
   Old Rose: $1/16$ tsp.
   Wild Rose: $1/32$ tsp.
B. *The same soft pink going to yellow (a lovely swatch!).*
   Dye values 1, 2, and 3 in Yellow: $1/32$ tsp.

Oranges.

A. *A pastel orange.*
   Peach: $1/4$ tsp.
B. *The same pastel orange with pink overtones (lovely!).*
   Dye all values in Wild Rose: $1/32$ tsp.

A. *A fairly bright rust-orange.*
   Rust: $1/4$ tsp.
B. *The same rust-orange, but definitely subdued.*
   Dye all values in Brown Rust: $1/32$ tsp.

Yellows.

A. *A deep gold to a nice yellow.*
    Buttercup Yellow: $1/4$ tsp.
    Mummy Brown: $1/32$ tsp.
B. *The same yellow-gold with brown overtones.*
    Dye values 4, 5, and 6 in Mummy Brown: $1/32$ tsp.

A. *A very bright lemon yellow.*
    Yellow: $1/4$ tsp.
B. *A lemon yellow, but not quite so bright (this is better!).*
    Dye values 4, 5, and 6 in Medium Brown: $1/128$ tsp.

Neutrals. Since the first value in a neutral swatch will be white, the sixth value of dye formula is not used.

A. *A white swatch with dark values of pale yellow.*
    Maize: $1/32$ tsp.
B. *The same white with dark values of brown for depth.*
    Dye values 4, 5, and 6 in Medium Brown: $1/128$ tsp.

A. *A lovely white swatch going to a taupe-green.*
    Silver-Gray-Green: $1/32$ tsp.
    Old Rose: $1/128$ tsp.
B. *The same white with a lavender overtone (I can't resist this shade).*
    Dye all values in Lavender: $1/128$ tsp.

A. *A white swatch going to khaki drab.*
    Khaki Drab: $1/16$ tsp.

Greens.

A. *A very usable yellow-green.*
    Bronze-Green: $1/4$ tsp.
    Buttercup Yellow: $1/64$ tsp.
B. *A yellow-green with noticeably more yellow in light values.*
    Dye values 1, 2, and 3 in Buttercup Yellow: $1/16$ tsp.

A. *A nice blue-green.*
    Reseda Green: $1/4$ tsp.
    Silver-Gray: $1/32$ tsp.

B. *A blue going to blue-green.*
    Dye values 1, 2, and 3 in Blue: $1/128$ tsp.

A. *A grayed olive-green.*
    Olive Green: $1/8$ tsp.
    Canary: $1/16$ tsp.
B. *An unbelievable color formed by adding Strawberry.*
    Dye all values in Strawberry: $1/32$ tsp.

Brown.

A. *A brown swatch is always useful.*
    Medium Brown: $1/8$ tsp.

Dip-Dyeing

Dip-dyeing is quite different from dyeing six-value swatches; the colors are dyed on a single piece of wool with dark shades at one end of the fabric and light shades at the other. The wool strip can be dyed shades of one color or shades of two or three colors.

Dip-dyed material has many uses. It makes a lovely hooked leaf, and it lends itself to a number of flowers, such as tulips, poppies, and irises. Apart from flowers, dip-dyed wool is effective for hooking scrolls or basket-weave designs in borders.

Equipment Needed

Dyes. Cushing dyes are used in all of these formulas.

Wool flannel.

Two enamel or stainless steel pans. Use 2-quart pans.

Tongs.

Large stirring spoons.

Glass 1-cup measuring cup.

Dye spoons. Triple Over Dye (TOD) measuring spoons work well. These spoons measure 1/4 teaspoon at one end and 1/32 teaspoon at the other end.

Set of aluminum measuring spoons.

White vinegar. Vinegar acts as an agent to set the color.

Rubber gloves.

Electric kettle.

Basin for soaking wool.

Paper towels and newspaper to protect table surfaces.

Preparation of Wool

You can use white or off-white wool, or you can include pastel wools to give a wider range of colors.

Cut the wool into 3-inch-by-18-inch pieces. Soak the wool in water and a little dish detergent overnight or for at least four hours. You will dye four pieces at a time.

Method of Dyeing

1. Fill one pan half full of *hot* water. Bring the water to a boil, and then turn it down to simmer.

2. Select the dyes for the specific formula you want to use. Mix with boiling water in a 1-cup measuring cup. This is the dye formula.

3. Add the amount of dye formula required.

4. Add 1/8 cup of vinegar, and stir.

5. Put on your rubber gloves to protect your hands from the hot water. You will be holding the top of the wool strip as you dip it into the dye.

6. Hold four pieces of wool at one end. Lower the strips about 4 inches into the dye bath.

The secret to dip-dyeing is to keep the wool moving up and down to avoid getting a definite line of color on the wool strips. The final result should produce a smooth transition from a light shade to a darker shade. At first, move the wool up and down while keeping the bottom third of the strips in the dye bath; then gradually immerse the strips until two-thirds of each strip is in the water. Keep the wool strips separated by moving them from one hand to the other.

Note 1. When you are dyeing strips a single color from dark to light, drop the four pieces of wool into the pan before the water clears. The end of the wool that was held will be the light end. Simmer the wool for 10 minutes before removing it. Then rinse the wool and let it dry.

Note 2. When you want to use another color at the top end of a strip of wool, remove the wool from the dye bath and place it in the sink. Use the second pan to dye the top end. You can add the correct amount of dye directly to the water in the pan. Stir the dye into the water, and add 1 tablespoon of vinegar.

Hold the wool strips by the dark ends and lower them into the dye bath so that about one-third of each strip is in the water. A small portion of the dyed wool, as well as the undyed ends, will be immersed. Remove the wool to the sink when the water is clear or when the wool is the color you want. Rinse the wool and dry it.

Note 3. To make the dark ends of the wool strips even darker—or to add a third color—follow the directions in Note 2 with one exception. Dip the *dark* ends of the wool, rather than the light ends, into the dye bath.

Dip-Dyeing Formulas

Use four pieces of 3-inch-by-18-inch wool with these formulas. Mix the first dye in 1 cup of boiling water and use all of it. If you want to use a second or third color, you can put the dye directly into the dye bath.

Note: The first dye in each of the following formulas can be used alone to produce a single-colored piece of wool, shading from dark at one end to light at the other.

Scarlet: $1/8$ tsp.
Buttercup Yellow: $1/32$ tsp. for top third of wool strip
Plum: $1/32$ tsp. for bottom third

Crimson: $1/8$ tsp.
Plum: $1/32$ tsp. for bottom third

Buttercup Yellow: $1/8$ tsp.
Pink: $1/32$ tsp. for top third
Plum: $1/32$ tsp. for bottom third

Purple: $^1/_8$ tsp.
Old Rose: $^1/_{32}$ tsp. for top third
Plum: $^1/_{32}$ tsp. for bottom third

Formulas for leaves.

Bronze Green: $^1/_8$ tsp.
Dark Green: $^1/_{32}$ tsp. for bottom third

Silver-Gray-Green: $^1/_4$ tsp.
Dark Green: $^1/_{32}$ tsp. for bottom third

Bronze Green: $^1/_8$ tsp.
Buttercup Yellow: $^1/_{32}$ tsp. for top third
Dark Green: $^1/_{32}$ tsp. for bottom third

Silver-Gray-Green: $^1/_4$ tsp.
Cardinal: $^1/_{32}$ tsp. for top third
Dark Green: $^1/_{32}$ tsp. for bottom third

Roses

Chinese lanterns, Queen Anne's lace, buttercup, chrysanthemum, silver dollar, cosmos

Nasturtium, foxglove, hibiscus, petunia, hollyhock, primrose, peony

Orchid, poinsettia, camelia, holly

Sweet pea, daisy, lupin, geranium, calla lily, poppy, tiger lily

Morning glory, Canterbury bells, pansy, aster, iris, anemone

Violets, pussy willow, tulip, daffodil, magnolia, lilac

Columbine, lily of the valley, jack-in-the-pulpit, crocus, trillium, hepatica, dogwood

Spot Dyeing

Throughout this book you have probably noticed that spot-dyed wool has been suggested for stems, veins, and even separation of petals. Spot-dyed wool is exactly that, wool with a variation of colors, achieved by spooning three or four dyes onto the crumpled wool.

Equipment Needed

Dyes. Cushing dyes have been used in these formulas.

Wool Flannel. Use white, off-white, or any light colored wool such as yellow, beige, light green, light blue, gold, or pink.

Pan. A low cake pan would be ideal, 9 inches square or 9 inches by 12 inches.

Glass 1-cup measuring cup.

Three or four glass jars. The dyes will be mixed in these.

Dye spoon.

Measuring spoons.

White vinegar.

Basin for soaking wool.

Electric kettle.

Rubber gloves.
Paper towels.

Preparation of Wool

Rip the wool into 3-inch-by-9-inch or 3-inch-by-18-inch pieces. Soak these in the basin for at least four hours.

Method of Dyeing

1. Crumple the pieces of wool into the pan.
2. Select the dyes for the specific formulas you want to use. Measure the correct amount of dry dye for each formula into a separate glass jar. Add 1 cup of boiling water and 1 tablespoon of vinegar to each jar, and stir.
3. Pour 3 tablespoons of one dye formula onto a single spot on the crumpled wool. Repeat this at random spots.
4. Do the same with the other dye formulas, pouring each onto a different spot. Don't worry if some of the colors overlap. Use a spoon to push any undyed wool down into the dye formula.
5. Cover the pan with foil and place it in a 250-degree oven for one hour. Remove the wool from the pan, rinse it, and dry it. Notice the glorious combination of colors.

Dye Formulas

Veins and stems.
Golden Brown: ¼ tsp.
Dark Brown: ¼ tsp.
Taupe: ¼ tsp.

Veins and stems.
Gold: ¼ tsp.
Medium Brown: ¼ tsp.
Mummy Brown: ¼ tsp.
Dark Brown: ¼ tsp.

Autumn leaves.
Gold: ¼ tsp.
Cardinal: ¼ tsp.
Rust: ¼ tsp.
Olive Green: ¼ tsp.

Autumn leaves.
>   Terra Cotta: ¹/₄ tsp.
>   Nile Green: ¹/₄ tsp.
>   Buttercup Yellow: ¹/₄ tsp.
>   Turkey Red: ¹/₄ tsp.

Have fun creating your own color combinations. Remember, when you start with a variety of light-colored flannels, you end up with an assortment of wonderfully colored spot-dyed wools.

Dyeing an Antique Black Background

Instead of using black wool from the bolt for a dark background, try dyeing wool an antique black. It will make a wonderful difference in the overall appearance of your hooked rug.

Equipment Needed

Wool flannel.
One 4-quart enamel or stainless steel pan.
A TOD measuring spoon.
Set of aluminum measuring spoons.
White vinegar.
Rubber gloves.
Electric kettle.
Basin for soaking wool.
Paper towels and newspaper to protect table surfaces.

Preparation of Wool

Collect equal amounts of black wool and dark-colored wool that you have on hand (kelly green, scarlet, purples, blues, dark checks, and dark plaids). Soak the wool for at least two hours.

The wool can be used in pieces of any size.

Method of Dyeing

Use as much wool as you can comfortably fit into your pan. Cover the wool with hot water and bring the water to a boil. Then reduce the heat and simmer the wool for 15 minutes. As the wool simmers, the dark colors will bleed and mingle until the wool and water are both very dark. Add 1/4 cup of vinegar, and simmer the wool for another 15 minutes. Then remove the wool from the pan. Rinse the wool well and dry it. Cut all the wool into strips; mix the strips randomly before hooking.

If you find that the wool is not dark enough when you remove it from the pan, add 1/2 teaspoon of dry dark green dye directly into the water. Before you replace the wool in the pan, stir the dye well. Add 1/4 cup of vinegar and simmer the wool for 15 minutes. Then remove the wool, rinse it, and dry it.

Drying and Pressing of Flowers

When hooking a floral piece, you may sometimes want an actual flower in front of you as a model. Dried or pressed flowers work especially well: they retain their original beauty and last a long time. Why not pick some of your annuals or perennials and dry or press them for future use as guides for shading your hooked rug or as part of an attractive arrangement for your home?

Most flowers can be dried, but the following turn out particularly nicely: ageratum, aster, Canterbury bells, carnation, cockscomb, cornflower, cosmos, dahlia, daisy, larkspur, lupin, marigold, pansy, rose, snapdragon, snow-on-the-mountain, sage, and zinnia.

Silica gel, a crystaline compound with the capacity to absorb up to forty percent of its weight in water, is used to dry the flowers. The basic sugarlike crystals are mixed with larger crystals that have been impregnated with a nickel compound that changes from blue to pink when wet. This color change signals that the silica has absorbed all the water it can.

Equipment Needed

One cake tin with lid.
Silica gel.
Masking tape.

Method of Drying

1. Strip all leaves from the selected flowers and examine their stems. If the stems are fragile, remove them; you can add false stems later.

2. Pour enough silica gel into the cake tin to create a 1½-inch layer on the bottom.

3. Place the flowers face up or with clusters flat on top of the silica gel. Arrange the flowers so that they do not touch each other.

4. Gently sprinkle more silica gel over the flowers until they are completely covered.

5. Place the lid on the tin and seal it in place with masking tape. Do not disturb it for four to seven days, depending upon the thickness of the flowers. Thicker flowers like zinnias dry much more slowly than thinner ones such as daisies.

6. When the flowers are dry, carefully brush away the covering silica gel and remove the blossoms from the cake tin. These flowers can be stored in decorative glass jars—with one or two preserving teaspoonfuls of silica gel—or made up into arrangements. To arrange them, you might need to add new stems made from florist wire wrapped with green floral tape. Whether in jars or arrangements, the dried flowers are ready as visual guides for that floral rug you are hooking.

Before reusing the silica gel, you must dry it in a warm oven—about 30 minutes at 250 degrees—until the pink crystals turn blue again. These should be stored in an airtight container such as the cake tin to prevent them from absorbing moisture from the air.

Remember when you pressed your first corsage between the pages of a large book? Now you can press flowers properly in just a few days. Naturally flat flowers work best, but any that you choose should be picked at their prime and have their stems removed.

Equipment Needed

One board large enough to hold your flowers.
White blotting paper.
White facial tissue.
Silica gel.
One plastic bag that will fit over the board.
Several bricks or heavy books.
Masking tape.

Method of Pressing

1. Cover one side of the board with a sheet of blotting paper and thin layer of silica gel. Place an even layer of tissues over the silica gel.

2. Arrange the flowers on the tissues so that none of the petals touch one another.

3. Cover the flowers with another layer of tissues, a layer of silica gel, and finally a sheet of blotting paper.

4. Carefully slide the board and its contents into the plastic bag, leaving the bag unsealed.

5. Place the entire package on a firm, level surface such as a hardwood floor or countertop. Gently position the weights—bricks or books—on top of the plastic bag. Squeeze the excess air from the bag and seal it with masking tape. Do not disturb the package for one week.

6. Carefully remove the pressed flowers from the surrounding layers of paper, silica gel, and tissues.

You can use pressed flowers to make beautiful gifts such as greeting cards, bookmarks, or wall plaques. If you press more flowers than you immediately need, you can store the extra ones between sheets of tissue in an airtight plastic container.

The Flowers

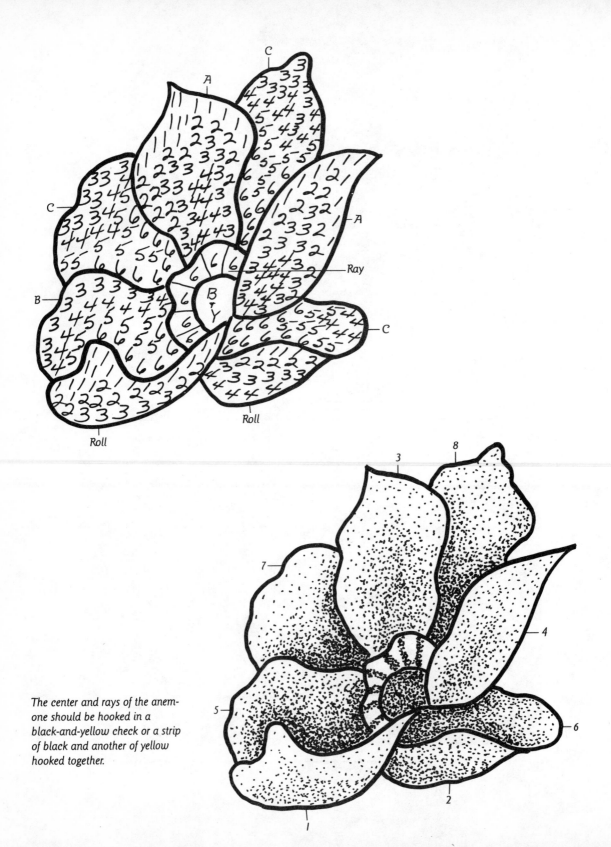

The center and rays of the anemone should be hooked in a black-and-yellow check or a strip of black and another of yellow hooked together.

Anemone

The anemone is commonly called the wind flower. The anemone is rich in historical associations. Biblical scholars tell us that the lovely *Anemone coronaria*, known as St. Brigid's anemone, is the "lily of the field" referred to in the Bible.

Flower Shape

An open-petaled flower with large petals.

Color

Pink, white, mauve, or red.

Order of Hooking

Center. To hook the center of the flower, use a black-and-yellow check or use a strip of black and a strip of yellow together. Starting with the center circular portion, hook rays out from the center in the same colors. Each ray will be an end-loop-loop-end. (After you hook the rolls on the petals, go back and hook the spaces between the rays with value 6.)

Petals. Hook the first roll in light values, starting at the lower edge of the petal with value 3 and shading to value 1. The second roll will still be light, but shade it with value 4 where it goes under the first roll. Then starting with the bottom edge, shade with values 3, 2, and 1.

Hook the first A petal with value 4 at the center base (where the base of the petal meets the center of the flower) and shade out to value 1. Shade the second A petal the same way. Follow the illustration for the placement of colors.

Make the B petal dark at the center base and where the petal goes under the roll. Begin with value 6 and shade out to value 3 or 2.

The first C petal is covered on one side by a roll and on the other side by an A petal, so it will be quite dark. Start with value 6, shading out to value 3. The second and third C petals are covered on both sides by other petals. You can hook them the same way you hooked the first C petal.

Leaves. The anemone leaves are curled and parsleylike. Hook them in a yellow-green.

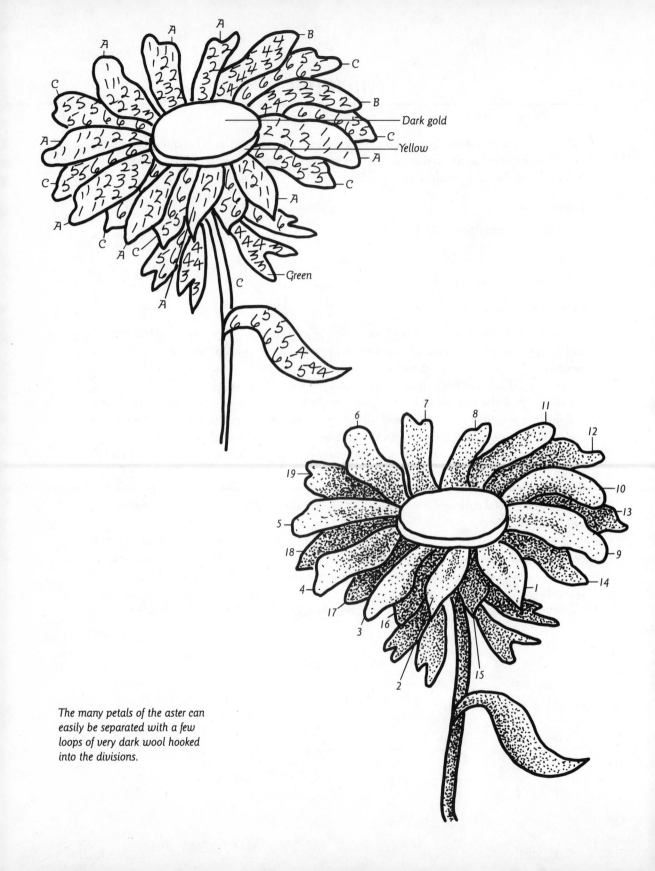

Dark gold

Yellow

Green

The many petals of the aster can
easily be separated with a few
loops of very dark wool hooked
into the divisions.

Aster

There are many distinct kinds of asters classified by their individual flower structures. Asters can be annuals or perennials. They make a fine cutting flower from midsummer until late frost.

Flower Shape

An open-petaled flower with an abundance of narrow petals.

Color

Pink, crimson, red, purple, blue, and white.

Order of Hooking

Center. The center of the aster is a disk. Hook the middle in gold and the edge in yellow.

Petals. There are nineteen petals: ten A petals, two B petals, and seven C petals. You will want to keep the A petals light, so that there will be a noticeable contrast with the B and C petals. Hook the petals in order, following the numbers given with the shaded illustration, to obtain the finished aster you want. Try not to pack your loops as you hook. And remember that there are four green sepals underneath the petals.

Leaves. The aster has long, narrow leaves that require only two or three values of color. You can hook them in a yellow-green or in a true green.

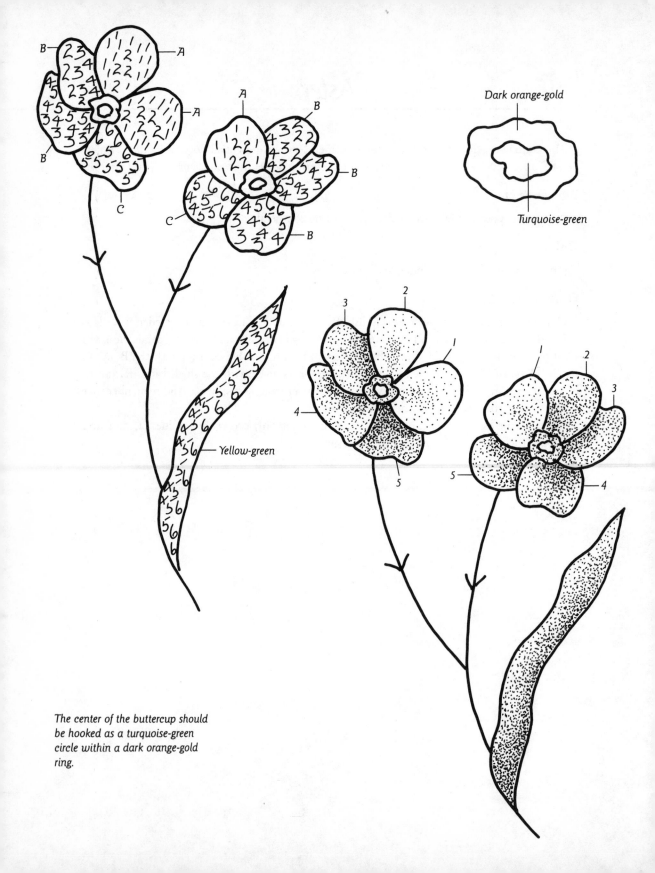

Dark orange-gold

Turquoise-green

Yellow-green

The center of the buttercup should
be hooked as a turquoise-green
circle within a dark orange-gold
ring.

Buttercup

There are some sixty species of buttercup. Buttercups can be found in fields or tended gardens; they grow as creepers, as erect plants, and even as water plants. But they all have shiny yellow petals.

Flower Shape

An open-petaled flower with small petals.

Color

Bright yellow.

Order of Hooking

Center. Hook the inner circle in the center a light turquoise-green, and hook the outer circle an orange-gold.

Petals. Begin by hooking the A petal in the flower on the right; hook it in values 2 and 1. Hook the B petal in values 4, 3, and 2, starting at the edge where the petal goes under the next petal. Hook one of the remaining B petals in values 5, 4, and 3, and the other in values 6, 5, 4, and 3. Since the petals are so small, it is important to skip at least one value between a light and a dark petal. Hook the C petal in values 6, 5, and 4, starting at the edges where the petal goes under the other petals.

Hook the flower on the left in the same order, but notice that this flower has two A petals, two B petals, and one C petal.

Leaves. The long, narrow leaf is easy to hook. Make the stem brown, and use the stem color along the lower edge of the leaf about two-thirds up the leaf. Mock shade the leaf with any green you choose, shading from one side of the leaf to the other side. Extend each value past the previous shade. To ensure a nicely shaded leaf, hook the rows of shading on a pleasant curve with no straight lines.

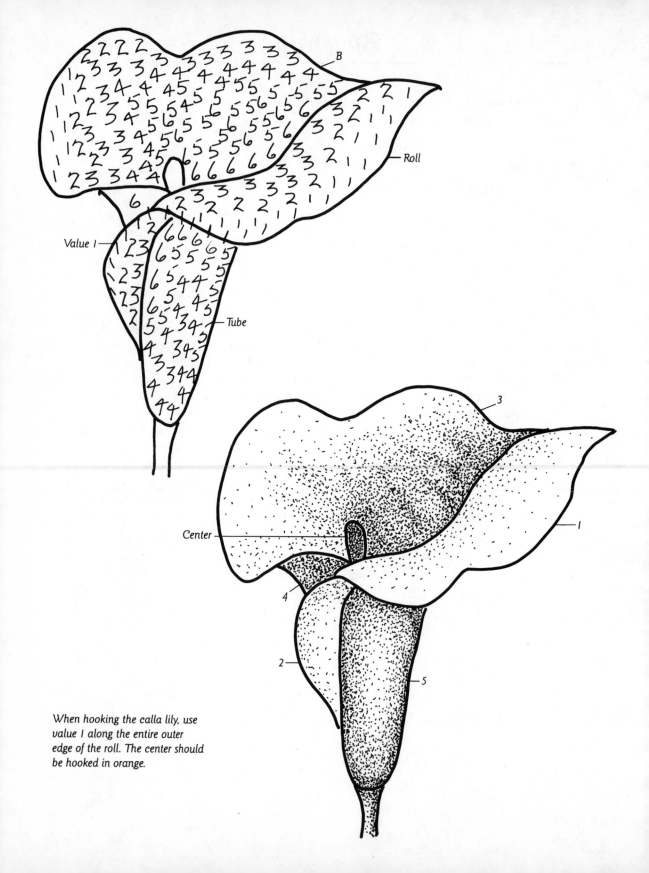

When hooking the calla lily, use value 1 along the entire outer edge of the roll. The center should be hooked in orange.

Calla Lily

Many people think of the calla lily as a florist's flower, but callas grow easily in any garden. Planted in groups of five or more, they create a stunning visual effect with a bright splash of white.

Flower Shape

A tube-shaped flower.

Color

A white swatch that goes to a light gray-green.

Order of Hooking

Center. The center is orange.

Petals. Hook the long rolled petal, shading from value 3 at the top of the petal to value 1 at the lower edge. You will need more than one row of each value. Add a bulge—extra loops—of value 3 to prevent the appearance of straight rows. If you hook an end-loop-loop-end along the middle of the previous row, the following rows will have a curved appearance. Hook value 1 on the lower left edge of the rolled petal and carry it along the left edge of the lower part of the roll. Shade the lower part of the roll at the tube edge with value 3; shade the rest of the area with value 2.

To hook the B petal, you will need more than one row of each value. Use value 6 to hook the center base and the edge where the petal goes under the roll. Also use value 6 to hook three fingers of varying lengths. Make the finger on the right by hooking an end-loop-end, the middle finger by hooking an end-loop-loop-end, and the finger on the left by hooking an end-loop-loop-loop-end. Keep the fingers curved. Follow these fingers with the remaining values, remembering to repeat the values where necessary.

To hook the tube, hook value 6 under the rolled petal and down the left side of the tube. Follow with values 5, 4, and 3, making a slight shadow of value 4 at the base and value 5 on the right edge of the tube.

Hook the last small area of the flower with value 6.

Leaves. The leaves of the calla lily are large and arrow-shaped. Choose a dark green swatch for hooking the leaves.

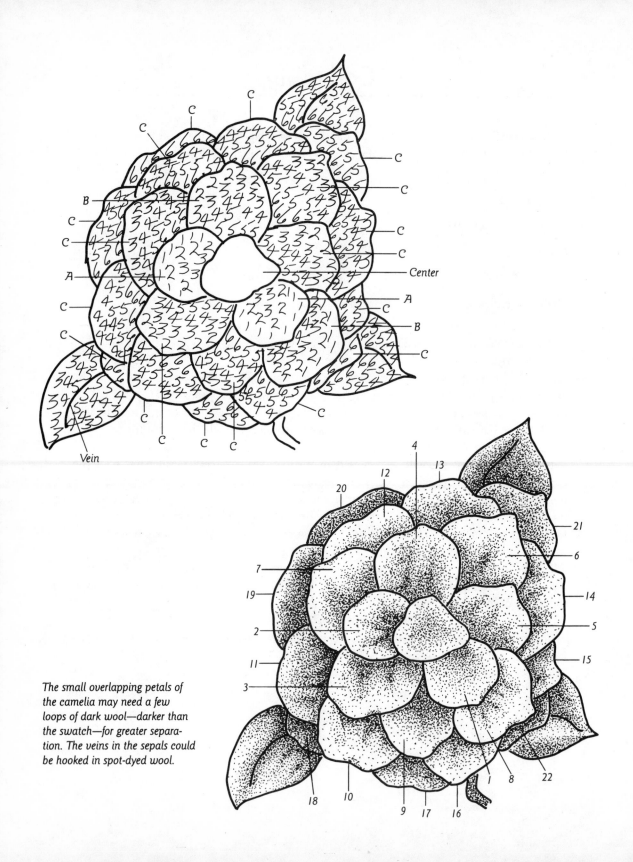

The small overlapping petals of the camelia may need a few loops of dark wool—darker than the swatch—for greater separation. The veins in the sepals could be hooked in spot-dyed wool.

Camelia

The camelia is an exotic greenhouse plant, although it is also grown successfully outdoors in the southern United States. The camelia's romantic appeal is confirmed by its wide use in corsages.

Flower Shape

An open-petaled flower with small overlapping petals.

Color

White, light pink, and deep rose.

Order of Hooking

Center. Hook the center in gold and brown. A check or plaid in these colors would be ideal.

Petals. The petals are placed in circles around the center. Make them light in color. Use values 3, 2, and 1 for the inner petals; the outer petals will be darker.

When you hook small overlapping petals, try hooking the dark value first, then the light value, and then the medium value. This order will give you more control over the edges of the petals. As you hook, keep an eye on the surrounding petals so you will know how light to go for a good contrast.

Leaves. The leaves of the camelia are a dark, rich blue-green.

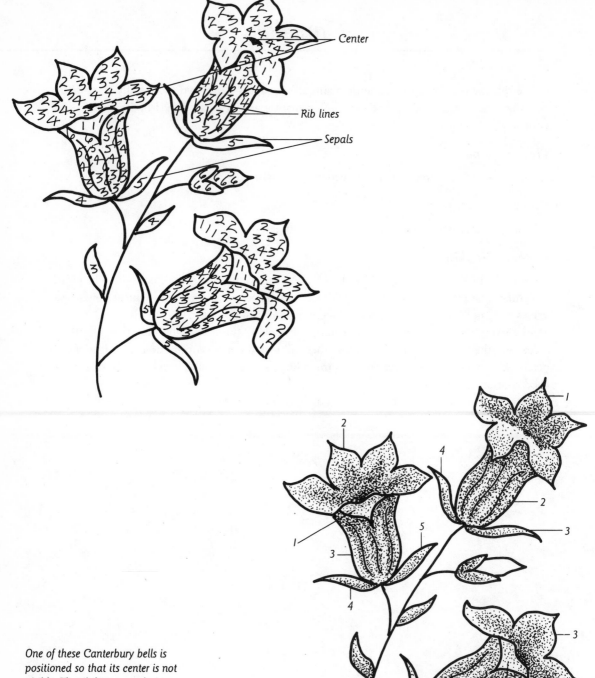

Center

Rib lines

Sepals

One of these Canterbury bells is positioned so that its center is not visible. The rib lines must be very dark—value 6—to add detail to the tubes.

Canterbury Bells

This flower is also known as campanula or simply as a bell flower. The name *Canterbury bells* may allude to the horse bells once used by the pilgrims visiting St. Thomas à Becket's shrine in Canterbury Cathedral. There are more than three hundred species of Canterbury bells; they appear everywhere from rock gardens to perennial beds. The flowers, which bloom for a long period of time, are extremely popular with gardeners.

Flower Shape

A medium-size bell-shaped flower.

Color

Pink, white, blue-mauve, and purple.

Order of Hooking

Center. The first flower to be hooked—the flower on the right—has no center. The flowers on the left and at the top have yellow-green centers.

Petals. Follow the illustrations carefully, noting the order of hooking and details of shading. To hook the flower on the right, notice the two petals that roll forward; hook these petals in the two lightest values. Make the three petals in back slightly darker by using value 4 at the center base, shading out to value 1.

Make the rib lines on the tube very dark; use value 6. Shade the top of the tube under the front petals with value 5, shading down the tube to value 3. Make the sepals at the base of the tube green in value 5.

To hook the flower on the left, first hook its center, making it yellow-green, and then hook the rolled front petal in value 1. Hook the shadow under the center with value 5, shading out to value 2 at the edge of the four petals. Hook the tube in the same way you did the tube of the flower on the right. Make the sepals green—the left sepal in value 4 and the right sepal in value 5.

To hook the top flower, begin by hooking its center in yellow-green. Begin shading above the center with value 4, going to value 2. Hook values 2 and 1 below the center. Hook the tube as you did before. Hook the left sepal in value 4 of green and the right sepal in value 5.

Hook the bud in values 6 and 5 of your flower swatch. Hook the base of the bud in value 6 of green.

Leaves. This beautiful plant has long, rough, wavy-edged leaves. Choice of color could be a true green or a slightly grayed green.

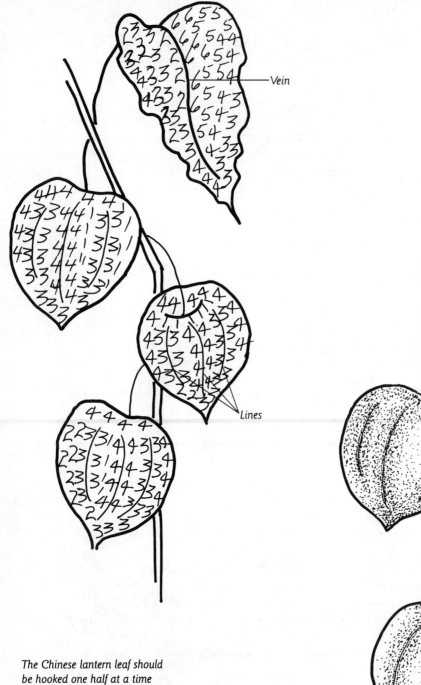

Vein

Lines

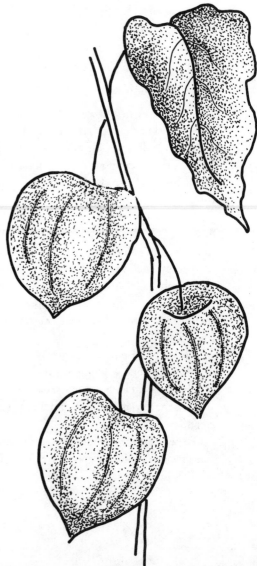

The Chinese lantern leaf should be hooked one half at a time using a yellow-green swatch. The lanterns can be hooked in any order.

Chinese Lantern

The Chinese lantern is valued for its balloonlike orange-red seed coverings, which resemble miniature Chinese lanterns. There is an edible, but bitter, scarlet berry inside each lantern. You can easily dry the lanterns to use in winter bouquets. Pick them in the fall just as the lanterns turn red, remove the leaves, and hang them by their stems upside down in a shady, well-ventilated location.

Flower Shape

An oval or round shape.

Color

Shades of orange. Use orange dye and add a small amount of medium-brown dye to the final two values.

Order of Hooking

Lanterns. Hook three curved lines in medium-brown on each lantern. Use value 4 on either side of the middle line and value 3 on either side of the two outside lines. Follow the illustration to complete each lantern with the correct values.

Stems. Hook the stems in brown spot dye or in dark values of medium-brown.

Leaves. We usually see the lanterns as decorative groupings in our homes. The plants have been dried and their leaves removed. In the garden the plants have large, long-stalked, yellow-green leaves.

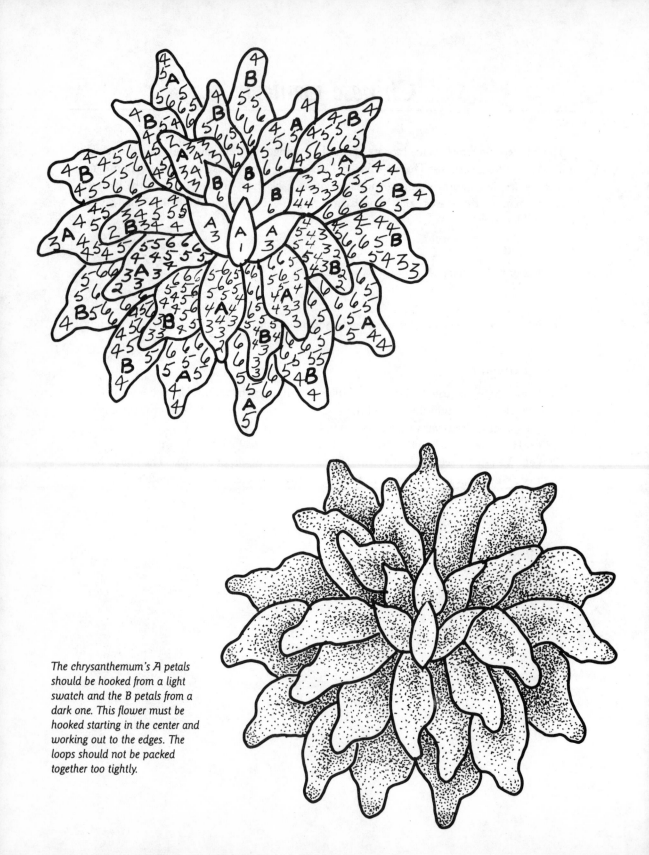

The chrysanthemum's A petals should be hooked from a light swatch and the B petals from a dark one. This flower must be hooked starting in the center and working out to the edges. The loops should not be packed together too tightly.

Chrysanthemum

The chrysanthemum has long been prized in the Far East. It was cherished by the Chinese philosopher Confucius. And some scholars believe that the red circle that dominates the Japanese flag represents a chrysanthemum rather than the rising sun. The chrysanthemum is widely cultivated for its attractive and long-lasting blossoms, which are available when other flowers are scarce.

Flower Shape

A many-petaled flower with narrow petals.

Color

Pink, yellow, white, orange, rust, gold, and wine. Since the petals of the chrysanthemum are so small, hook it with two swatches—a light, bright swatch and a dark, dull one—to make it appear more natural and to facilitate shading.

Order of Hooking

Petals. When you look at the illustrations for hooking the chrysanthemum, you will find that the positions of the A, B, and C petals and the numbers indicating the order of hooking have been omitted. In this case, you should hook the petals labeled A with the light swatch and the petals labeled B with the dark swatch. Start in the center of the flower and work out to the edges, carefully following the illustrations.

If the divisions between the small petals become difficult to see, use a strip of brown that is dark enough to contrast with the swatches used. Pull up a few loops between the petals until the desired effect is achieved.

Leaves. The chrysanthemum leaves are fairly large and deeply lobed in three sections. Choose a dark green or a yellow-green swatch.

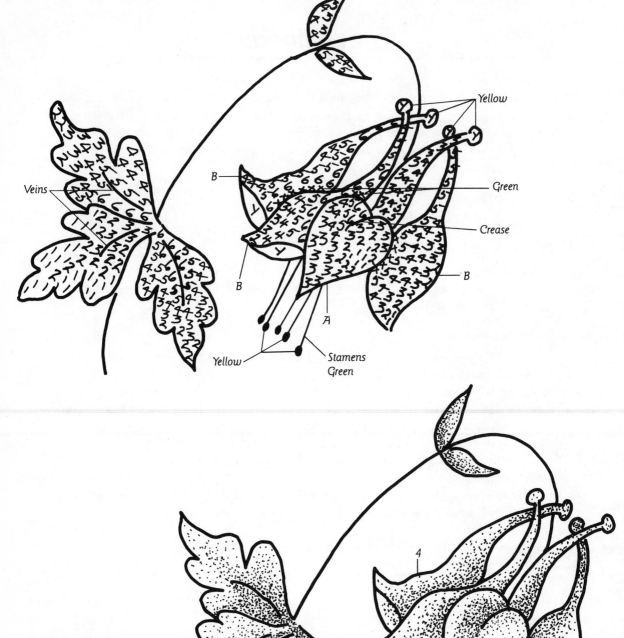

Veins

Yellow

B

Y

B

Y

B

A

Green

Crease

B

Yellow

Stamens
Green

4

3

1

2

The columbine's stem
is hooked in brown,
its petal knobs in
yellow, and its leaf
veins in any one of
the flower's colors.

Columbine

The columbine is a well-known flower, found in many different areas of the world, especially in European gardens. Once highly valued for medicinal purposes, the columbine has a long and respected history. This graceful flower blooms in middle and late spring, bearing an airy, distinctive flower high above clumps of deeply lobed, dark green or blue-green leaves.

Flower Shape

A tube-shaped flower with some irregular shapes.

Color

Red, pink, yellow, blue, lavender, and white.

Order of Hooking

Center. The center consists of yellow and green stamens with yellow dots. These hang down below the petals. Follow the illustrations for proper placement.

Petals. The A petal is shaped like a heart with a crease at the top. Hook the right side of the petal in light values 3, 2, and 1. Shade the left side in values 6, 5, 4, and 3. Use a medium green along the outer curve of the right side of the petal. This area is shown on the chart as XXXX. Shade the tube in values 5, 4, and 3, working from the bottom right to the top. Hook all of the knobs in yellow.

Shade the B petal on the right, including the tube. Begin with value 5, shading out to value 1 at the bottom of the petal.

Shade the first B petal on the left of the A petal, including the tube. Start with value 6, shading out to value 2 or 3. Hook an end-loop-loop-end of medium green along the left curve of the petal. Hook the small area at the base of the petal in a medium yellow.

Shade the last B petal, including the tube. Shade from the right side of the petal in values 6, 5, and 4. Hook the small area at the base of the petal in yellow.

Leaves. The leaves of the columbine are deeply lobed, dark green or blue-green.

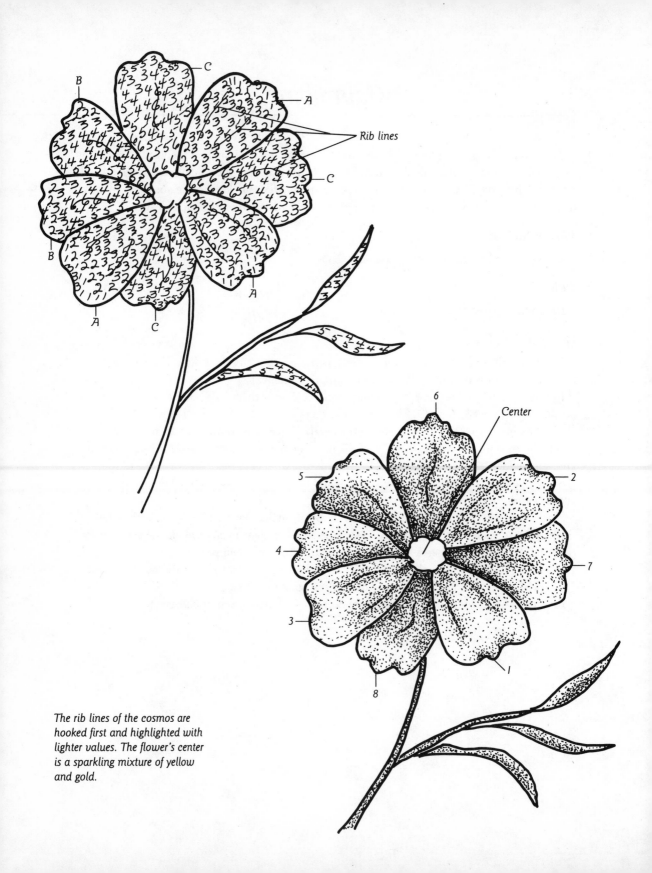

Rib lines

Center

The rib lines of the cosmos are
hooked first and highlighted with
lighter values. The flower's center
is a sparkling mixture of yellow
and gold.

Cosmos

The cosmos is a large flower, similar to a daisy, with large, overlapping petals. Its foliage is delicate and feathery. In its native habitat in Mexico, the cosmos matures rapidly, growing four to six feet high.

Flower Shape

A many-petaled flower with large, open petals.

Color

Rosy pink, white, mauve, or red.

Order of Hooking

Center. Hook the center in a mixture of yellow and gold.

Petals. There are three A petals. Notice the rib lines on each petal. Hook the rib lines first in value 5; then hook value 3 around the rib lines and at the base of the petals. Fill in the rest of each petal with value 2 and even with value 1 if there is enough space.

Hook the rib lines on the two B petals in value 6. Use value 5 along the edges where the petals go under another petal. Follow the illustrations carefully.

There are three C petals. Hook the rib lines in value 6. Shade the petals from value 6 at the base out to value 3.

Check the illustrations as you hook the ruffles at the ends of the petals, and remember to skip a value for the shadows. If you are using a pale swatch, you may need to darken the edges of the C petals. Just use a dark value from a flower nearby, hooking an end-loop-loop-end where the petals meet at the center.

Leaves. There are several narrow leaves on a single stem. Hook the leaves in a yellow-green, using mock shading.

The light A petal brings this
crocus to life above its dark
leaves.

Crocus

There are seventy-five species and innumerable varieties of crocus. During the Middle Ages, the saffron crocus was a prized source of drug and dye chemicals, as well as a flavoring agent. Saffron is obtained from the dried stigmas of crocus; it takes more than four thousand flowers to make a single ounce of saffron.

Flower Shape

A small, open-petaled flower.

Color

Mauve, pink, white, and purple.

Order of Hooking

Petals. The one A petal will be the lightest; hook it in values 3, 2, and 1. Hook value 3 at the base and up the middle as a finger, using an end-loop-loop-end. Widen the top of the finger by adding extra loops of value 3. Then hook values 2 and 1, remembering to extend each value at least two loops beyond the previous value. You may have to repeat one of the values on this petal.

There are three B petals. Begin with the first B petal to the left of the A petal. Use value 5 where the B petal goes under the A petal to hook a finger, using an end-loop-loop-end. Begin at the base of the petal and work towards the tip with values 4, 3, 2, and 1.

Hook the other two B petals in value 5 (and value 6) where the petals go under other petals. Then add values 4 and 3. Notice that there are no fingers in these two petals.

There are two C petals. Hook the C petal on the left in values 5, 4, and 3. Hook the other C petal in values 6 and 5.

To hook the crocus bud, begin with the A petal. Keep the petal fairly dark by hooking a finger, using an end-loop-loop-end with value 5, from the base of the petal. Add values 4 and 3. Then hook the two B petals in value 6 where the B petals go under the A petal. Add values 5, 4, and 3. Hook the C petal, where only the tip is visible, in value 6.

Leaves. The crocus has narrow, dark green leaves.

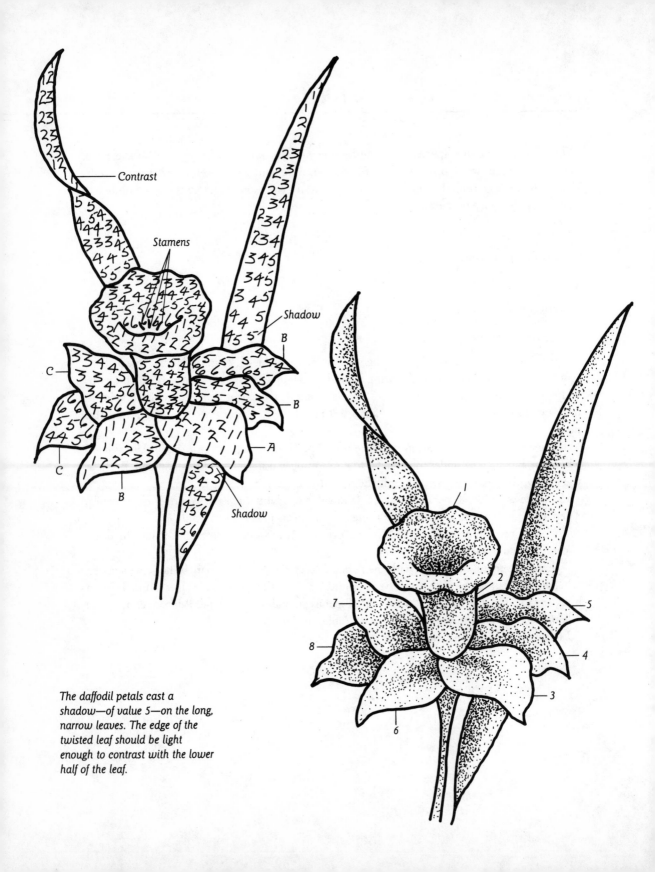

Contrast

Stamens

Shadow

B

C

B

C

B

Shadow

A

1

2

7

5

8

4

3

6

The daffodil petals cast a
shadow—of value 5—on the long,
narrow leaves. The edge of the
twisted leaf should be light
enough to contrast with the lower
half of the leaf.

Daffodil

The many forms of narcissus, commonly referred to as daffodils, are among the most popular of all spring-flowering bulbs. The daffodil consists of fairly large open petals with a "trumpet" in the middle. Daffodils are planted in broad masses for maximum visual impact.

Flower Shape

A tube-shaped flower with petals.

Color

Yellow petals and a yellow tube, or white petals and a yellow tube.

Order of Hooking

Center. The center contains green stamens.

Tube and Petals. Hook the flared mouth of the tube first, following the numbered illustration. If the curved line in the center of the tube is not dark enough to contrast well with the rest of the flower, try hooking in a little brown between the dark and light values. Unless the daffodil is fairly large, you may find that you won't have enough room to shade the ruffles. Complete the tube by shading under the flared mouth with value 5, shading to lighter values.

When you hook the petals, it is important to do them in order, carefully following the numbered illustration. If there is not enough contrast where the tube meets the petals, or between two petals, hook in an end-loop-loop-end of brown.

Leaves. Daffodil leaves are called "strap" leaves, because they are long and narrow. Hook them in a yellow-green. Hook the leaf on the right in mock shading—shading from dark on one side of the leaf to light on the other side. You need to create a shadow where the leaf goes under the petals. Hook a dark value two-thirds of the way up the side of the leaf. Then hook the next value beside it, extending it about four loops. Add the rest of the values.

Shade the twisted leaf on the left where it goes under the petals and where it goes under the turnunder. Hook the shadows in value 5. Then add values 4 and 3. Make the turnunder light, shading from value 3 on the right side to value 1 on the left.

Use a brown-green spot dye on the stem.

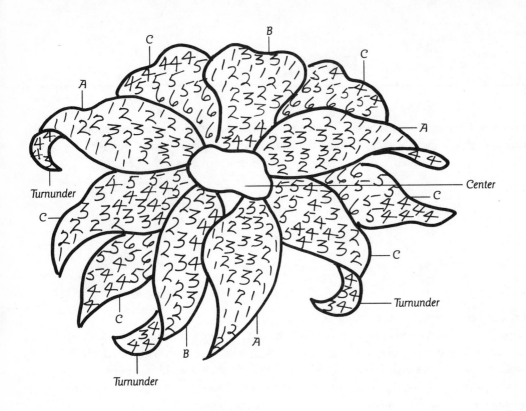

C

B

C

A

Turnunder

C

C

Turnunder

B

A

Center

C

C

Turnunder

A

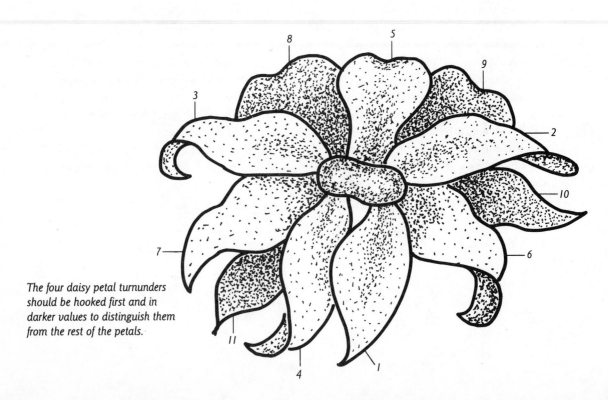

8

5

9

3

2

7

10

6

11

4

1

The four daisy petal turnunders should be hooked first and in darker values to distinguish them from the rest of the petals.

Daisy

Everyone is familiar with this delightful summer flower. Daisies grow profusely as wildflowers, and they also provide brilliant splashes of color in cultivated gardens. The daisy belongs to the largest family of garden flowers.

Flower Shape

A many-petaled flower with narrow petals.

Color

Yellow, white, pink, purple, orange, or red.

Order of Hooking

Center. The center of the daisy is dark brown.

Petals. Daisies are difficult to master, but hooking this one will be easier if you keep several points in mind. Begin by studying the positions of the petals. There are three A petals, two B petals, and six C petals. As you are hooking, keep an eye on the surrounding petals; each flower should have light petals on top and darker petals underneath.

Four petals have turnunders at the tips. Hook the turnunders before you do any of the petals. Use value 4 as the darker value on the outer curve of each turnunder and value 3 on the inner curve. You can use values 1 through 5 if the turnunder is large.

If you follow the order of hooking presented in the illustrations, you shouldn't have any trouble hooking a daisy. Remember that the swatch you use should have a definite contrast between light and dark values so that each petal will appear distinct.

Leaves. Daisy leaves are smooth and narrow. Hook them in a yellow-green.

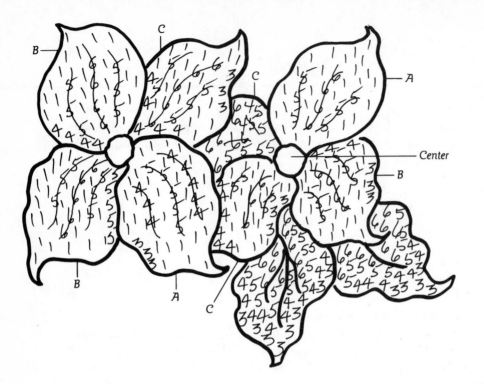

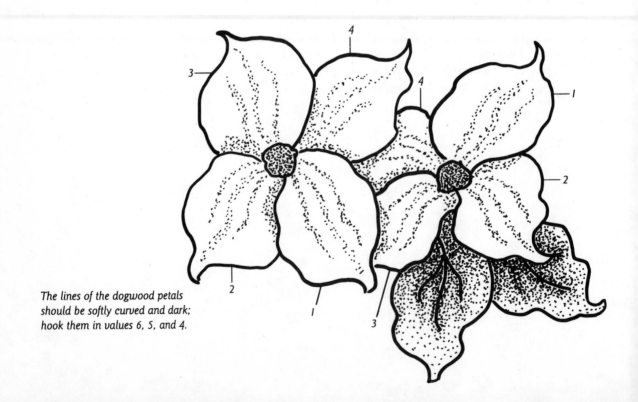

The lines of the dogwood petals should be softly curved and dark; hook them in values 6, 5, and 4.

Dogwood

The dogwood is famous for its grace and beauty—especially in the eastern United States. Each spring, the clusters of creamy white flowers create an unforgettable picture. The wood from dogwood trees was once used to make bows and arrows.

Flower Shape

An open-petaled flower with medium-size petals.

Color

White to silver-gray or the color of maize.

Order of Hooking

Center. Hook the center in a yellow-and-green tweed.

Petals. Hook the flower on top first, following the numbered illustration to determine the order of hooking. There are a few suggestions to keep in mind as you hook the dogwood flowers. Hook the lines in each petal in dark values 6, 5, and 4. Hook the lines in a pleasing curve; don't use any straight lines. Notice that all the B and C petals have a shadow where they go under other petals. Hook the ruffles where they are indicated in the illustration. Then hook the rest of each petal in value 1. Remember that the first value of a white swatch was not dyed, so if you need more of that value, simply add another piece of white wool.

Leaves. The dogwood leaves are a yellow-green. Follow the illustration for the correct placement of color.

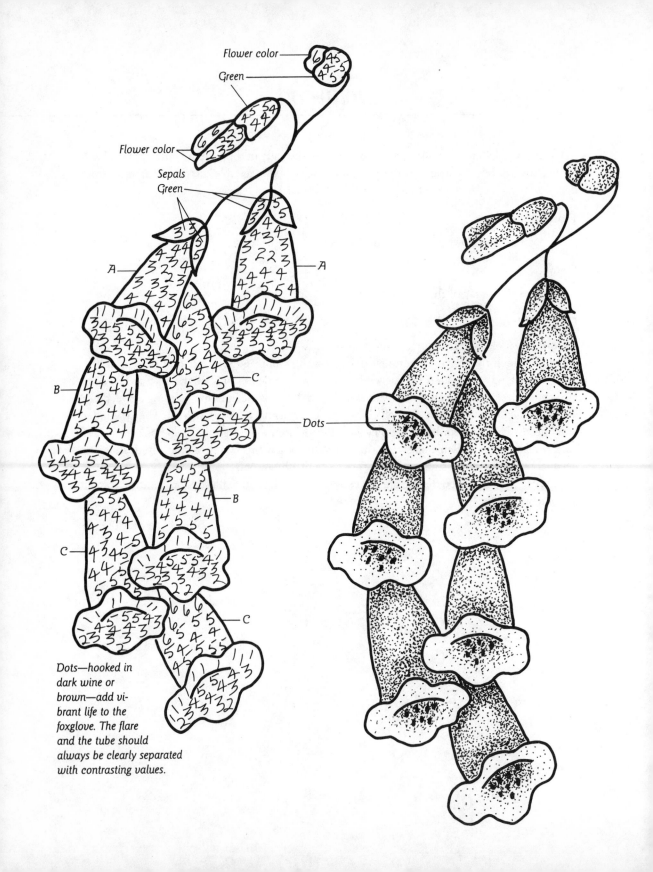

Flower color
Green
Flower color
Sepals
Green

A

B

C

Dots

Dots—hooked in
dark wine or
brown—add vi-
brant life to the
foxglove. The flare
and the tube should
always be clearly separated
with contrasting values.

Foxglove

Although the foxglove is native to Western Europe, it appears all over the world. The plants grow three to six feet tall and produce striking spikes of finger-shaped flowers. The flower's common name, in fact, derives from "folk's gloves." The heart stimulant, digitalis, comes from the dried leaves.

Flower Shape

A tube-shaped flower.

Color

Cranberry, purple, blue, yellow, or pink.

Order of Hooking

Center. Use a dark wine or brown wool to hook the dots in the center of each flower after the flower is completed. To make the dots, pull up an end and a loop; then pull an end through the same hole that was used for the first end. Don't forget to hook these dots, because they make the flower come alive.

Flowers. Hook the flowers at the top first; then go on to the ones underneath. Hook each flower, beginning with the lower part of the flared mouth. Hook down from the curved line in the center with values 5, 4, 3, and 2. Hook the upper part of the flared mouth with value 1. If the curved line in the center of the flower doesn't show up satisfactorily, hook about three loops along the curve in a dark color.

Hook the tube in value 5 to create a shadow where the tube meets the flared mouth and at the base of the tube. There must be a distinct separation between the flare and the tube.

Hook the sepals in green. Use dark values of green to hook the bases of the buds. Hook the buds with the flower color.

Leaves. Foxglove leaves are a silver-gray-green. They are oblong to lanceolate in shape.

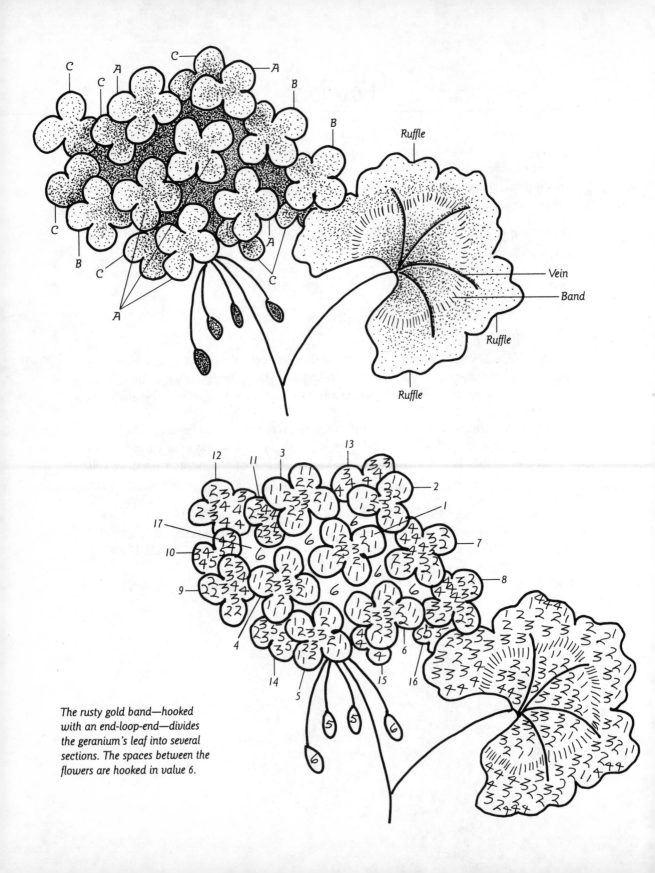

The rusty gold band—hooked
with an end-loop-end—divides
the geranium's leaf into several
sections. The spaces between the
flowers are hooked in value 6.

Geranium

The geranium is a popular flower that adds color to many gardens. Geraniums love full sunlight and bloom vigorously when other flowers are wilting.

Hooking a geranium is something like putting a jigsaw puzzle together: it's a little confusing at first, but it looks terrific when it's completed.

Flower Shape

An irregularly shaped flower.

Color

Vibrant red, coral, pink, and white.

Order of Hooking

Flowers. The small flowers are like little islands in a sea. Follow the illustrations carefully to determine the positions of the flowers and the order of hooking. After you complete the flowers, use the darkest value to hook all the spaces between them.

Leaves. The leaves of the geranium are almost as attractive as the flowers. The leaves are large and fan-shaped with fluted edges. You can hook them in blue-green, yellow-green, bronze-green, or a hunter green. Some varieties of geraniums have leaves with a rusty gold band dividing each leaf. The band divides the leaf into sections that can be hooked individually, making the leaf easier to hook. Hook the band first; then hook the veins.

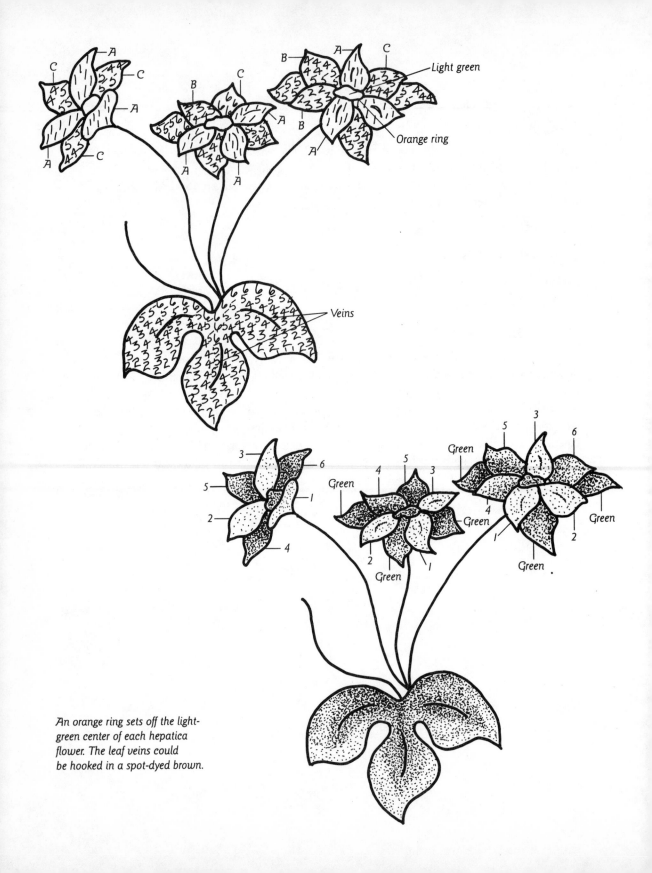

An orange ring sets off the light-
green center of each hepatica
flower. The leaf veins could
be hooked in a spot-dyed brown.

Hepatica

When spring arrives in the woods, so does the hepatica. The hepatica is a small plant with delicate flowers and ivylike leaves. It belongs to the buttercup family.

Flower Shape

An open-petaled flower with small petals.

Color

Lilac, blue, white, or pink.

Order of Hooking

Center. To hook the center, hook a ring of orange around a green center. Be careful; there is not much room!

Petals. To hook the flower on the right, hook the line in the three A petals with an end-loop-end of value 3. Hook the rest of each petal with value 1. Hook the first B petal with value 3 where it goes under the A petal. Fill remainder with value 2. Shade the second B petal where it goes under the petal below it with value 5. Then fill in the petal with value 4. Hook the C petal in values 4 and 3. Use a green swatch to hook the three sepals.

To hook the middle flower, begin by hooking lines in the centers of the A petals with an end-loop-end of value 3, filling in with value 1. Hook the B petal in values 4 and 3. Hook the C petal in value 6. Use a green swatch for the three sepals.

To hook the flower on the left, hook the three A petals in value 1 and the C petals in values 5 and 4. There are no sepals showing on this flower.

Leaves. Hepatica leaves have three lobes. Hook them in a bright green or dark green.

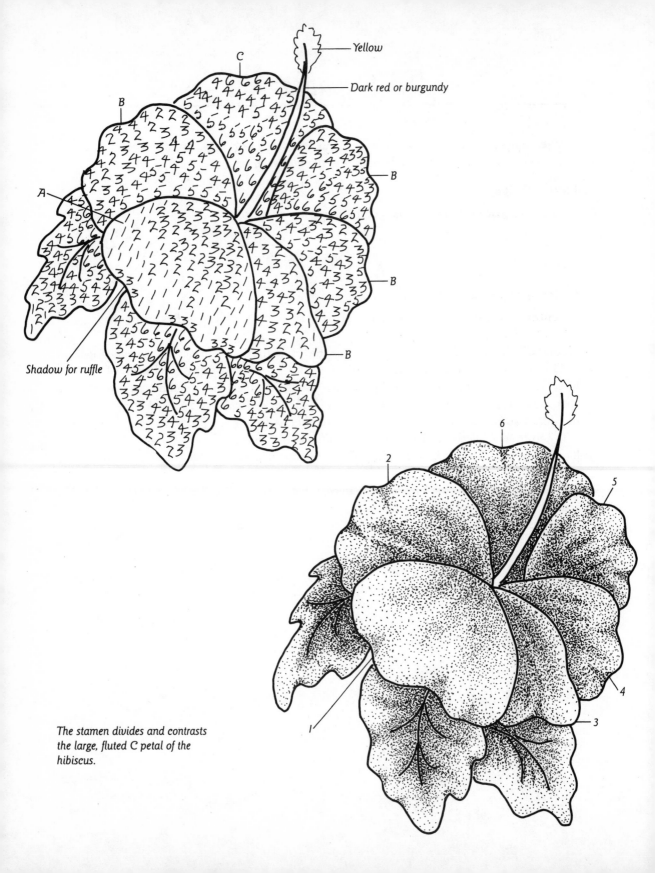

Yellow

Dark red or burgundy

Shadow for ruffle

The stamen divides and contrasts the large, fluted C petal of the hibiscus.

Hibiscus

The hibiscus grows in warm, tropical parts of the world; it must be grown under glass in temperate climates. Its large blooms, six to twelve inches in diameter, are highly cherished in Chinese gardens.

Flower Shape

A bell-shaped flower with large fluted petals.

Color

Red, pink, white, or yellow.

Order of Hooking

Center. The long stamen in the center of a hibiscus is usually dark red, but if the flower is red, hook the stamen in a middle value of green. The stigma at the end of the stamen is yellow.

Petals. This flower has one A petal, four B petals, and one C petal. The A petal is large and light in value. Hook four fingers in value 3 with an end-loop-loop-end. Follow with value 2, remembering to extend each value by two loops. Shade the edge of the fluted petal with value 3. Then hook the rest of the petal in value 1, following the fingers already in place.

Hook the B petal (to the left and above the A petal) in value 5 at the center base and where it goes under the A petal. Hook two fingers, using an end-loop-loop-end. Shade the fluted edge with value 4. Then fill in with values 4, 3, and 2, following the fingers.

To hook the B petal to the right of the A petal, use value 4 to hook a finger and also where the petal goes under the A petal. Shade out to value 1.

Hook the third B petal with value 5, shading out to value 2. Shade the fluted edge with value 5.

To hook the fourth B petal, use value 6 to hook a finger and to create a shadow where the petal goes under the petal below it. Shade out to value 2.

The dark C petal is divided by the stamen. Use values 6 and 5 on the right side of the stamen. Treat the left side as a separate petal. Use value 6 at the center base and where the petal goes under the stamen and under the other petal. Shade out to value 4, remembering to hook the shadow on the fluted edge with value 6.

Leaves. The hibiscus leaves are medium-size, small-lobed leaves. A sage green swatch would be a good choice.

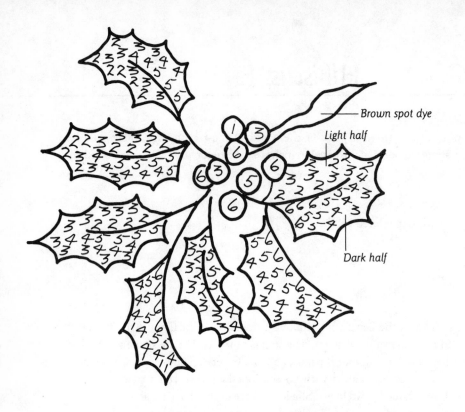

Brown spot dye

Light half

Dark half

These holly leaves—with their carefully hooked sharp points—can be done in any order. Mock shading divides them into light and dark halves.

Holly

Although there are many species of holly, the one most commonly hooked is the familiar Christmas holly that is seen in so many festive decorations. The dark green leaves and red berries are a recurring motif in many Christmas pieces.

Flower Shape

Holly has spiny leaves and round berries.

Color

The leaves are a glossy green; the berries are red.

Order of Hooking

Berries. Hook the berries first, keeping them the size they are drawn and using only one value per berry. Begin by pulling an end up in the center of the berry. Than hook three or four loops around the circle just inside the design line. Finally, pull an end up in the same hole that the first end was pulled through.

Leaves. Hook the stem and veins of the holly leaves, using a brown, a brown check, or a brown spot dye. Hook the leaves with mock shading by shading each leaf from the center vein out to the edges on both sides. Follow the illustrations that indicate the placement of values.

Be careful not to let the points on the leaves become rounded. If you have trouble, hook out to the point, cut the loop, and begin again just below the point. The points will be emphasized when the background is hooked around the leaf.

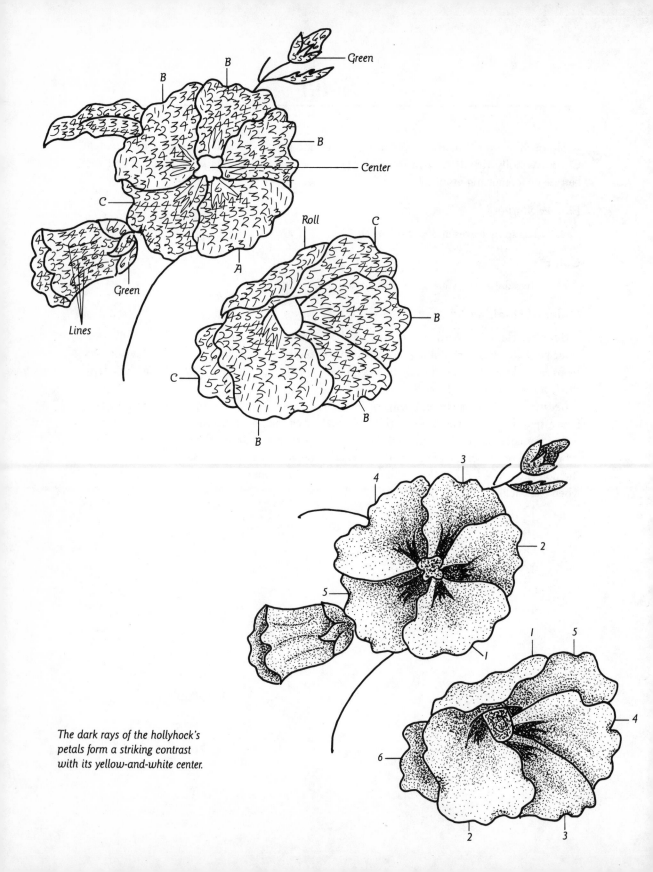

The dark rays of the hollyhock's petals form a striking contrast with its yellow-and-white center.

Hollyhock

The hollyhock, a favorite cottage garden flower, is indigenous to the Far East. It is a dramatic accent plant, especially when grown in rows against a wall or fence. The tall stalks bear numerous single and double flowers.

Flower Shape

A bell-shaped flower with large ruffled petals.

Color

Crimson, pink, mauve, maroon, and white.

Order of Hooking

Center. The center is a mixture of yellow and white.

Petals. The hollyhock petals have dark rays spreading from the center base of each petal. Use value 6 to hook the rays, and use value 4 next to the rays to emphasize them. Hook the shadows with value 5. Follow the illustrations carefully as you work.

To hook the flower on the right, first hook the roll in light values 3, 2, and 1. Then hook the B and C petals. To hook the flower on the left, hook the A petal, then the three B petals and the C petal.

When you hook the large bud, begin by hooking the three rib lines in value 6. Then shade the bud from value 5 at the base of the bud to value 2 at the ruffled edge. Hook the "inside" of the bud, seen at the top of the bud, in values 5 and 4. Hook the sepals in green.

To hook the small bud, use value 6 for the bud and green for the sepals.

Stem. Hook the stem in brown or in a brown spot dye.

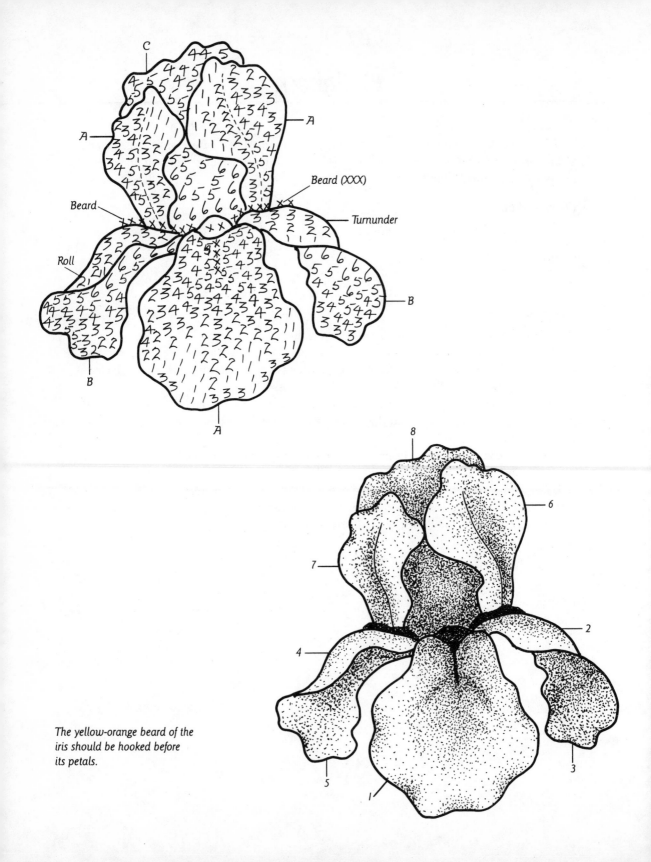

The yellow-orange beard of the iris should be hooked before its petals.

Iris

There are more than three hundred species of irises. The most popular is the German, or bearded iris. The superb flowers, which are large and shapely, are available in many colors and have a delightful scent. Irises can grow to a height of three feet.

Flower Shape

An irregularly shaped flower.

Color

White, yellow, bronze, mauve, burgundy, and blue.

You can hook an iris with either one or two color swatches. When using two, hook the three lower petals in one color swatch and the three upper petals in another color swatch or hook the three top petals and lower middle petal in one color swatch and the two lower side petals in another color swatch.

Order of Hooking

Petals. The "beard" of the iris is indicated by lines of Xs on the illustration. Hook the beard with yellow-orange. Shade the large A petal (the lowest petal) with value 5 at the base of the petal and on either side of the beard. Hook fingers of value 5 on an angle from the beard, shading out to the edge of the petal with values 4, 3, 2, and 1. Shade the ruffles of the petal by hooking darker values on the inner curves.

To hook the twisted petal on the right, hook the upper portion of the petal in light values 3, 2, and 1. Shade the lower portion at the twist with value 6. Hook a finger of value 6 with an end-loop-end, shading out to value 3.

To hook the petal on the left, hook the roll in values 3, 2, and 1. Shade the lower portion of the petal where it goes beneath the roll with value 6, shading out to value 2.

Now hook the two A petals at the top in the same way you hooked the lower petal. Notice the dashed line that divides each petal. By hooking dark values 5, 4, 3, and 2 on one side of the line and light values 3, 2, and 1 on the other side, you will create a pleasing visual division.

Keep the C petal very dark by hooking the lower portion of the petal in values 6 and 5 and the upper portion in values 5 and 4.

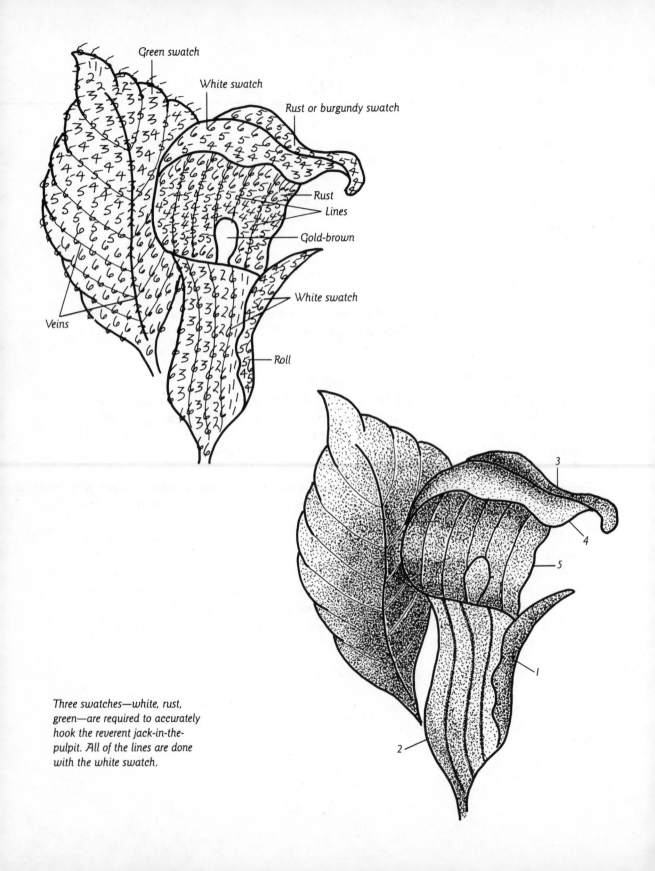

Green swatch

White swatch

Rust or burgundy swatch

Rust

Lines

Gold-brown

White swatch

Roll

Veins

Three swatches—white, rust, green—are required to accurately hook the reverent jack-in-the-pulpit. All of the lines are done with the white swatch.

3

4

5

1

2

Jack-in-the-Pulpit

The jack-in-the-pulpit is an American woodland wildflower that blooms in the early spring. It has an unusually dignified appearance.

Flower Shape

A tube-shaped flower.

Color

Use a white swatch and rust or burgundy.

Order of Hooking

Center. The center is a dull gold.

Flower. Hook the wrapped-around tube with a white swatch. Follow the illustrations carefully as you hook the vertical lines and the left edge of the tube in value 6. Then hook the spaces between the lines in values 1, 2, and 3. Use dark to medium values for the roll at the right of the tube.

Hook the upper portion of the hood's roll, shading outward with a rust swatch in values 6, 5, and 4. Hook the bottom portion of the roll with the white swatch, shading from the center with values 6, 5, 4, and 3.

Hook the vertical lines of the back of the hood with the white swatch, using three values to give it a rounded appearance. Begin with value 6, shade to value 4, and then work back to value 6. Shade the spaces between the lines in rust swatch, shading from value 6 to value 4 and back to value 6. Follow the illustrations carefully.

Leaves. Use a green swatch, a rust or burgundy swatch, and a white swatch. Hook the center vein with the white swatch; hook the side veins with the rust or burgundy swatch; hook the rest of the leaf with the green swatch. This is an unusual type of shading—almost an outline-and-fill technique—but the result is quite effective.

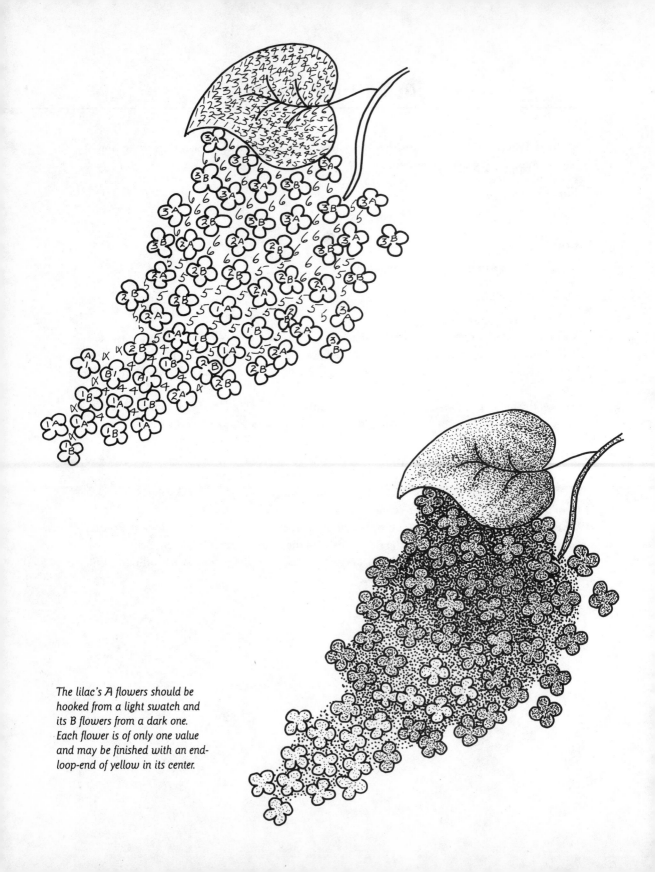

The lilac's A flowers should be
hooked from a light swatch and
its B flowers from a dark one.
Each flower is of only one value
and may be finished with an end-
loop-end of yellow in its center.

Lilac

A lilac bush has heart-shaped leaves and large bunches of little four-petaled flowers. The flowers bloom in early spring and are sweetly fragrant, especially after a shower.

Flower Shape

A cluster of open-petaled flowers with small petals.

Color

White, mauve, purple, yellow, and burgundy.

Order of Hooking

Center. When the flowers are completed, you can hook a loop of yellow in the center of each one if you like.

Flowers. The lilac is hooked differently from any other flower, so you will want to read the directions carefully before beginning. Choose two swatches that go well together—a light, bright swatch and a dark, dull one. Since the flowers are close together, using two different color swatches will help define the individual flowers.

In the illustration, one swatch will be indicated by A and the other swatch will be indicated by B. A flower labeled A1 should be hooked with value 1 of the A swatch. An A1 flower will have a B1 flower next to it, an A2 flower will have a B2 flower next to it, and so on.

You will hook each flower in a single value, and only values 3, 2, and 1 will be used for the flowers. The values will vary with the position of the flowers in the cluster: use value 3 near the stem, value 2 in the middle of the cluster, and value 1 at the tip of the cluster.

To hook the area behind the flowers, use the three darkest values from one of the swatches; use value 6 near the stem, value 5 in the middle of the cluster, and value 4 at the tip.

Leaves. The leaves of the lilac are heart shaped. Choose a dark green swatch and a medium brown for the veins. Follow the illustration to determine the correct placement of color.

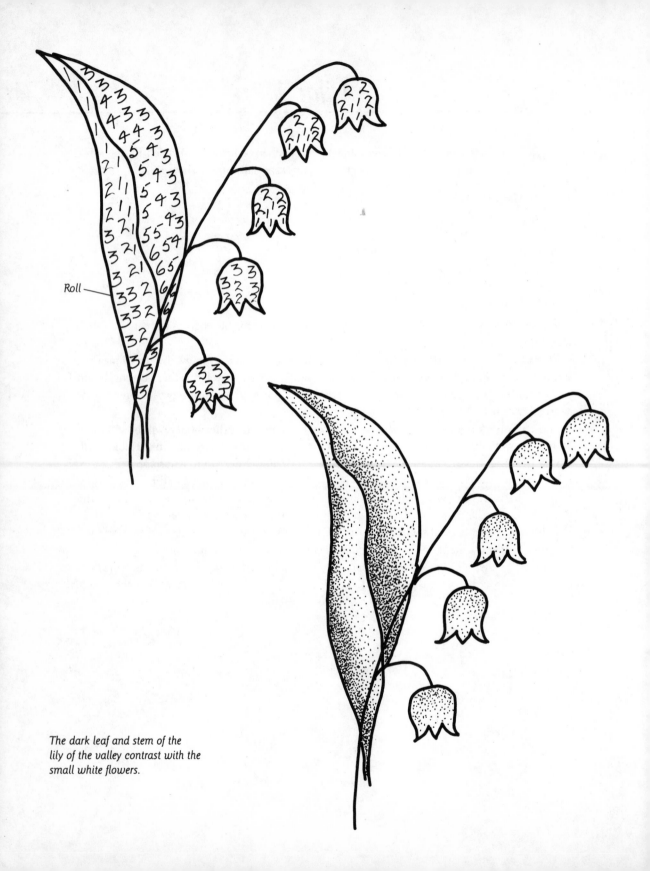

Roll

The dark leaf and stem of the
lily of the valley contrast with the
small white flowers.

Lily of the Valley

The lily of the valley, which has been cultivated for centuries in European gardens, is the national flower of Finland. When it blooms in the spring, the small white flowers give off a lovely scent. At one time, the roots of the lily of the valley were sold in apothecary shops for heart ailments. The bell-shaped flowers appeared frequently on medieval tapestries and other craftwork of that time.

Flower Shape

Small bell-shaped flowers with oval leaves.

Color

White.

Order of Hooking

Flowers. Use three values of white for each flower. (If the flowers you are hooking are larger than the ones in the illustration, you may want to use more than three values.) You can vary the use of the values, depending on the position of each flower on the stem. Don't be discouraged if the flowers look a little forlorn; they will be better defined after you complete the background.

Leaves. Hook the stem in a brown-green, and use a yellow-green for the leaves. Hook the roll on the leaf in light values. Then shade the rest of the leaf from the dark area beneath the roll to the light outer edge.

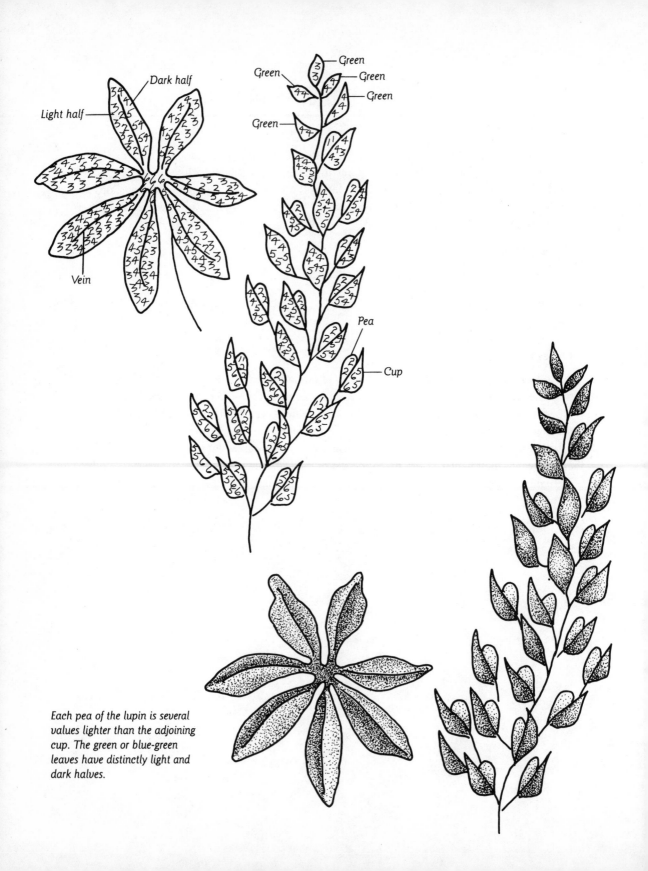

Dark half

Light half

Vein

Green
Green
Green
Green
Green

Pea

Cup

Each pea of the lupin is several values lighter than the adjoining cup. The green or blue-green leaves have distinctly light and dark halves.

Lupin

The lupin makes a colorful addition to any perennial garden. The flowers are spectacular spikes of closely set pea flowers; the leaves are palmlike, dark green on one half and light green on the other. The plants can grow up to thirty inches high.

Flower Shape

An irregularly shaped flower.

Color

Yellow, blue, purple, pink, red, or white.

Order of Hooking

Flowers. Each flower on the spike looks like a pea in a little cup. Begin by hooking the flowers at the base of the spike. First use two dark values for the cup; then use two light values for the pea. If you want to make the flower two colors, use one color swatch for the cup and another swatch for the pea.

The individual flowers will be darker at the base of the spike, gradually getting lighter near the top. Note that the flowers at the top of the spike are green.

Leaves. Use brown or brown spot dye for the stem and for the veins in the leaves. Hook the leaves in a true green or blue-green. Hook one side of the leaf dark at the vein, shading out to a lighter value at the edge of the leaf. Hook the other side of the leaf light at the vein, shading out to a darker value.

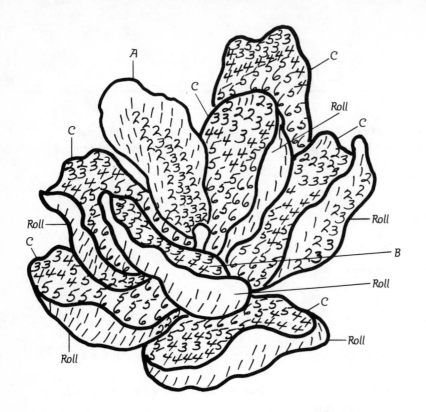

White highlights the many rolls of magnolia petals.

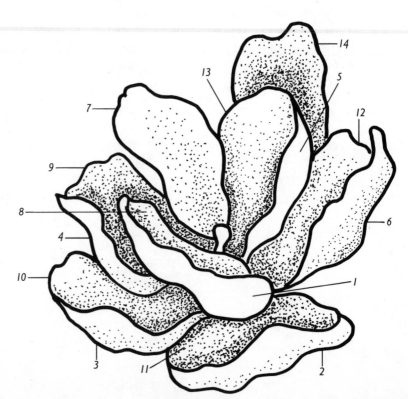

Magnolia

Botanists consider the magnolia to be one of the oldest trees or shrubs in the world. Magnolias bloom in the spring, creating a breathtaking display of enormous white flowers. The flowers are readily identified by their heady fragrance.

Flower Shape

An open-petaled flower with large petals.

Color

White to soft pink.

Order of Hooking

Center. The center is a rusty green.

Petals. This magnolia is a lovely flower to hook, perhaps because of its soft colors or the six curving rolls. Note that the blank spaces on the illustrations indicate areas that should be hooked in white. Hook the roll on the right in values 3, 2, 1, and white. Hook the remaining rolls in value 1 and white. Follow the illustrations carefully as you hook.

Hook the A petal in light values 3, 2, and 1. Hook the B petal in values 4, 3, and 2. Make the six C petals dark at the center bases and where the petals go under other petals. Hook the ruffled areas on the edges of the rolls and petals two values darker than the value around them.

The magnolia looks difficult to hook, but it is really easy and most enjoyable.

Leaves. The magnolia has large, oval leaves that are a glossy green.

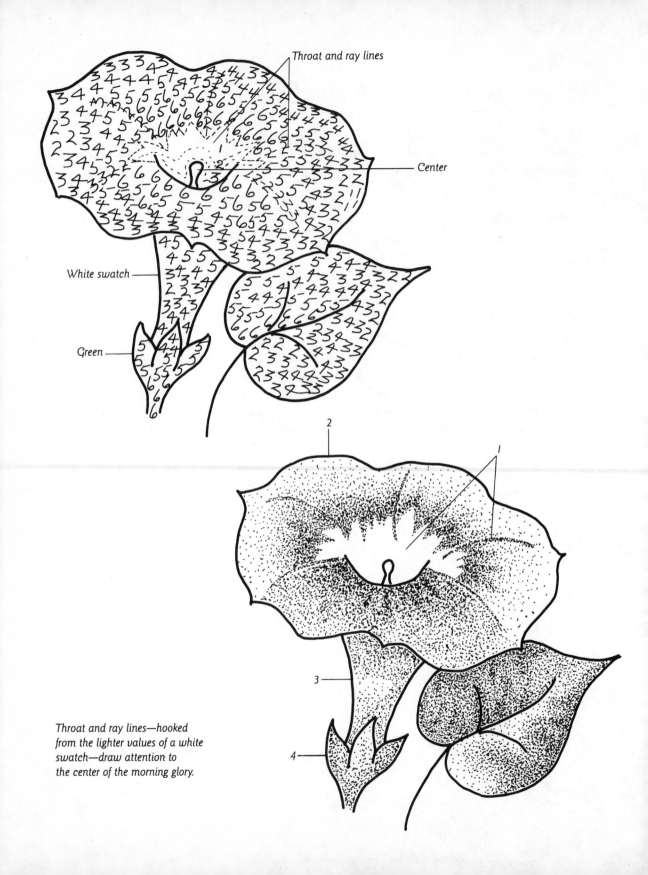

Throat and ray lines

Center

White swatch

Green

2

1

3

4

Throat and ray lines—hooked
from the lighter values of a white
swatch—draw attention to
the center of the morning glory.

Morning Glory

There are over five hundred species of morning glories. Originally native to tropical regions, morning glories are now found throughout much of the world. The large flowers and heart-shaped leaves are found in profusion, climbing on trellises, arbors, fences, and porches.

Flower Shape

A funnel-shaped flower.

Color

Azure blue, wine red, white, purple, and pink.

Order of Hooking

Center. The center is yellow. As you hook the center, keep it small.

Flower. Hook the mouth of the flower (around the center) in a white swatch with values 3, 2, and 1. Hook the five ray lines with a white swatch, beginning with value 2 and then using value 3. Don't hook the ray lines completely to the edge of the flower. Hook each section of the flower between the ray lines, shading from dark values near the mouth of the flower to light values at the outer edges. Follow the illustrations carefully to determine the placement of colors, and use fingers to extend the colors.

Hook the tube of the flower in a white swatch, following the illustrations as you work. Hook the sepals with dark values of a green swatch.

Leaves. Hook the vein of the heart-shaped leaf in brown or in the value of the flower color. Shade the right side of the leaf with a light value at the vein, shading to two values darker before returning to a light value. Shade the left side of the leaf with a dark value at the vein, shading to two values lighter before returning to a dark value for the shadow.

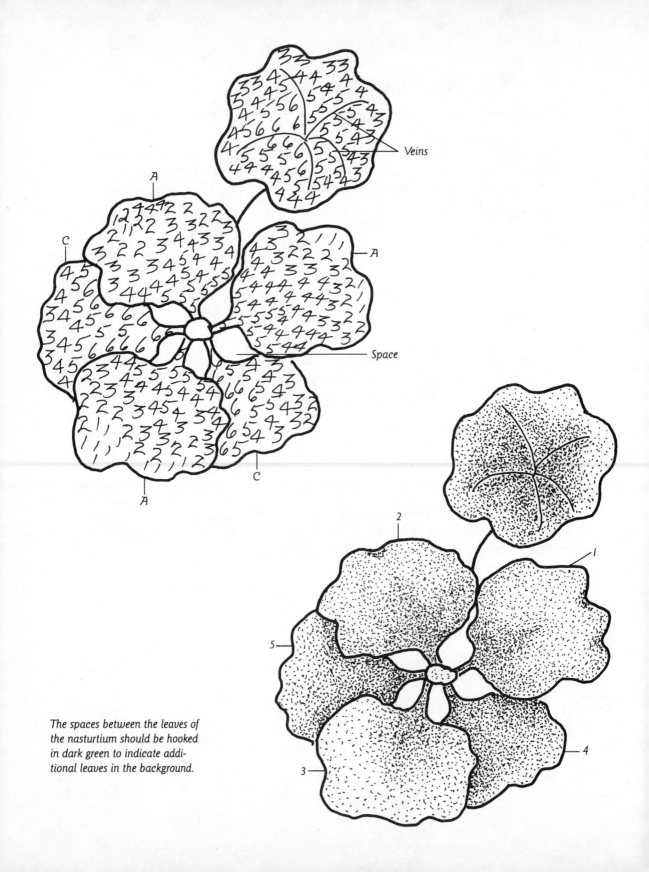

Veins

A

C

A

Space

C

A

2

1

5

4

3

The spaces between the leaves of
the nasturtium should be hooked
in dark green to indicate additional leaves in the background.

Nasturtium

Nasturtiums grow vigorously. They are capable of covering large areas. Nasturtiums were once cultivated as a salad staple. The leaves are tasty on sandwiches, and the flowers can be eaten in salads. Nasturtiums provide ten times as much vitamin C as lettuce.

Flower Shape

An open-petaled flower.

Color

Scarlet, crimson, maroon, rose, salmon, and white.

Order of Hooking

Center. The center is yellow or a mixture of yellow and gold.

Petals. Hook the three A petals in value 5 at the narrow base of the petal, shading out to the lightest value. Hook in a finger of value 5 with an end-loop-loop-end. Shade the ruffled edges of the petals on the inner curves of the petals, using a shade two values darker than the surrounding values.

Hook the two dark C petals with value 6 at the narrow base of the petal, shading out to value 3.

Note the pear-shaped spaces at the center of the flower. These are spaces where you can see through to the background behind the flower. If the background of your rug is light and if you hooked the light color in these spaces, you would create five bright stars that would detract from the flower. I recommend that you hook the spaces in dark green to give the impression that there are additional green leaves behind the flower.

Leaves. Hook the veins in the round nasturtium leaf in a light green. Hook the leaf in a yellow-green. Since the veins divide the leaf into five sections, hook each section separately as if it were a C petal. Follow the illustrations to determine the placement of colors.

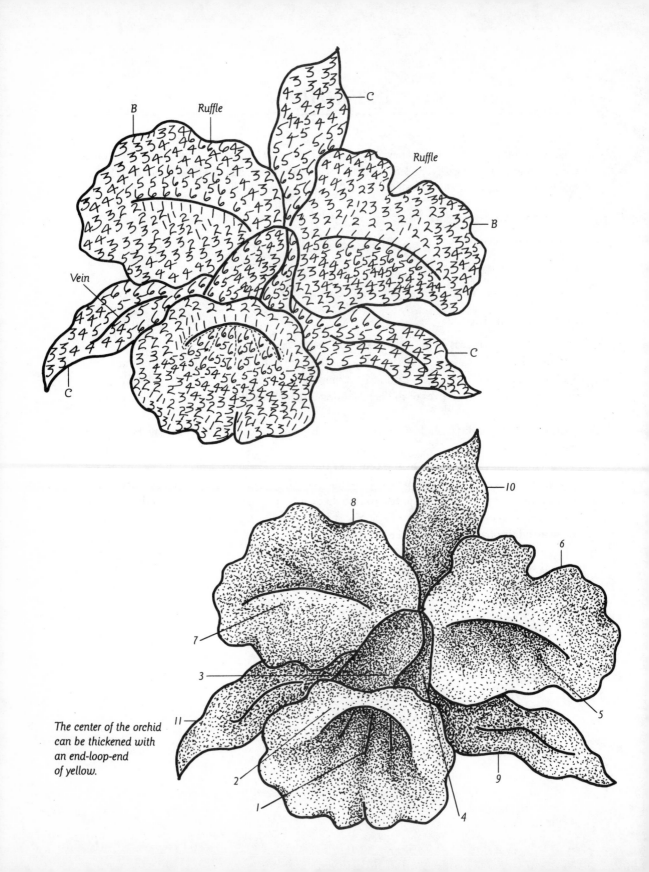

The center of the orchid can be thickened with an end-loop-end of yellow.

Orchid

Of almost twenty thousand species of orchids, only one hundred and sixty grow in North America. The orchid has three large showy petals with the middle petal modified into a conspicuous lip that secretes nectar. Despite the claims of numerous legends about orchids, they do not trap insects or people and are not known to have any medicinal value.

Flower Shape

The orchid includes a tube-shaped flower, ruffled petals, and narrow, leaflike petals.

Color

Blue, mauve, purple, white, yellow, pink, and red.

Order of Hooking

Center. The center is a yellow curve thickened at the ends; it has three yellow stamens.

Petals. First hook the flared mouth, beginning with value 6 below the yellow curve and between the yellow stamens in the center. Shade out with values 5 and 4. Hook the ruffled area on the edge in value 3. Now go back and finish with values 3, 2, and 1. Hook the area above the center in values 2 and 1.

Hook the wraparound tube next. On the left side of the tube, hook value 3 next to the wraparound line, shading out to value 6 at the edge of the tube. On the right side of the tube, use dark values 6 and 5.

Notice the two large ruffled petals, each with a definite line down the center. These petals are reversed in their shading: shade the ruffles along the inner curves with shades that are two values darker than the surrounding values. Follow the illustrations to determine the placement of fingers going out from the center lines.

Shade the three C petals at the center base and where they go under other petals. These are dark petals, shading from values 6, 5, 4, and 3.

Leaves. Orchids have pairs of broad leaves. Choose a true green swatch.

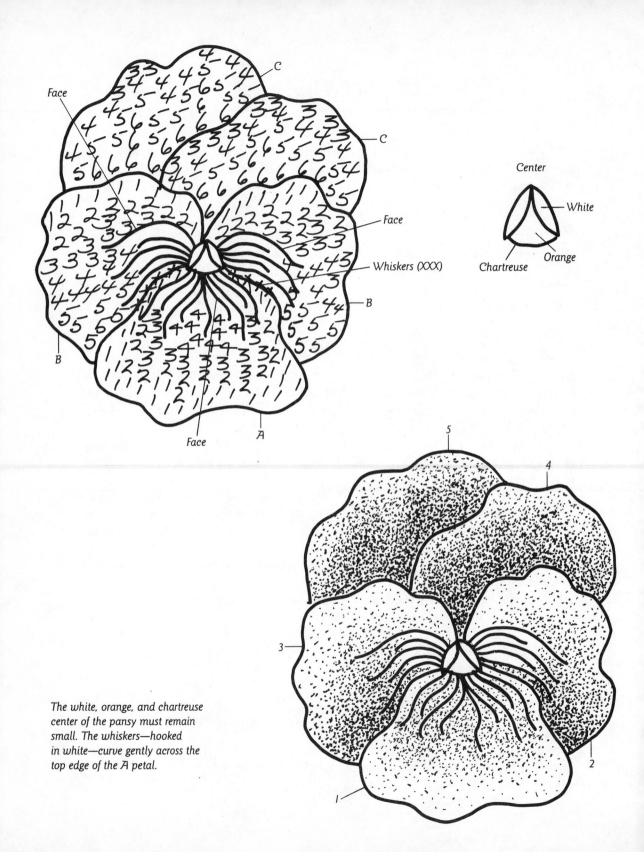

The white, orange, and chartreuse center of the pansy must remain small. The whiskers—hooked in white—curve gently across the top edge of the A petal.

Pansy

Pansies belong to the viola family. They make excellent border plants or massed plantings in perennial gardens. Pansies are a special favorite because of their distinctive markings.

Flower Shape

An open-petaled flower with large petals.

Color

White, blue, purple, red, orange, apricot, or yellow.

The pansy can be hooked in a wide range of colors with varying petal schemes, including: (1) the use of one color swatch, making the face dark, the three front petals light, and the two back petals medium to dark; (2) the use of two colors, hooking the face and the two back petals in one color and the three front petals in another color: and (3) the use of two colors, hooking the face in one color and all of the other petals in another color.

Order of Hooking

Center. As you hook the center, don't pack the loops or the center will become too big. Three colors are used: white, chartreuse, and orange. See the illustration for enlargement of center.

Petals. Hook the whiskers in white along the top edges of the A petal. The whiskers are indicated by Xs on the illustration, the face by solid lines. Note that the face appears in three petals. If you are hooking the face in values from a swatch, use value 5 to hook the face in the A petal and value 6 to hook the face in the B petals. Hook the face like a fan—with a long line and then a short line. Keep the lines nicely curved.

Begin hooking the A petal in the center of the petal, working value 4 up into the face. Follow the numbered illustration, making sure to hook values 2 and 1 up between the whiskers and the face.

To hook the two B petals, begin where they go under the A petal, and then again between the lines of the petals' faces. Shade these with values 5 through 1.

The two C petals will be much darker than the other petals. Begin by hooking two fingers with value 6. Do not shade out any lighter than value 3, even if it means repeating a value to keep the petals dark.

Leaves. Pansy leaves are medium sized. You can hook them in yellow-green. Use brown spot-dyed wool or another flower color for the veins.

The areas around and between the irregularly spaced peony petals are hooked in value 6.

Peony

The red shoots of peonies emerging from the ground have signaled the beginning of spring for generations. The peony, which has been known to live for thirty years, has an unforgettable fragrance and is excellent for cutting. It is native to parts of China, Siberia, and Japan.

Flower Shape

An irregularly shaped flower.

Color

Snowy white to pale yellow, and many shades of pink to serpent red.

Order of Hooking

Petals. In the peony, all the A petals are small. Hook them with value 2 at the center of the petal and value 1 completing the petal.

Shade the B petals where they go under an A petal, using values 3, 2, and 1, or in some cases, values 4, 3, 2, and 1. Shade the C petals with dark values where they go under other petals, shading out to medium values.

Hook the remaining area around the petals in value 6. This is an irregularly shaped flower, and the shading will also be irregular. Follow the illustrations carefully as you work.

Leaves. The peony has abundant fernlike leaves. Choose a true green for the leaves.

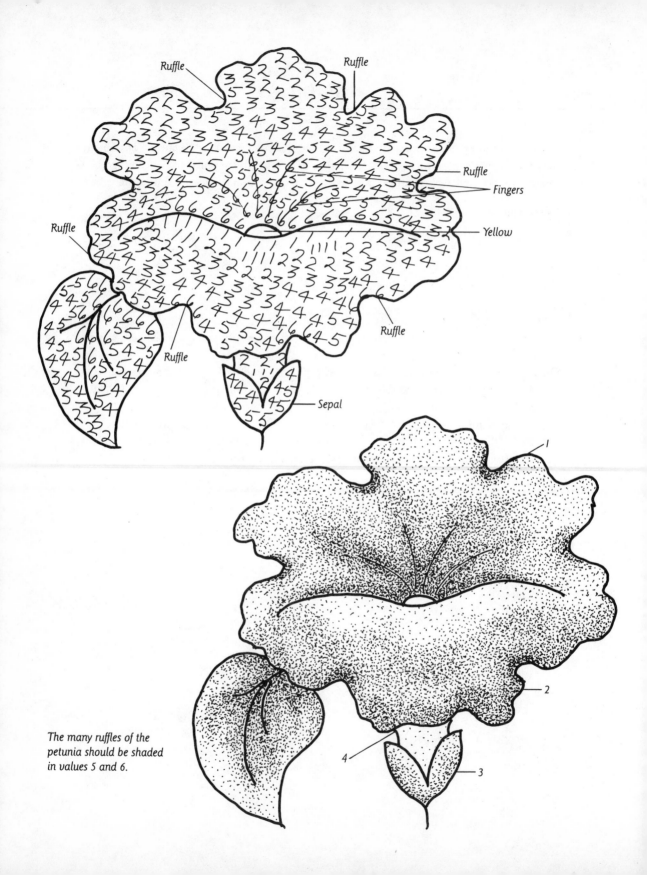

Ruffle

Ruffle

Ruffle

Fingers

Ruffle

Yellow

Ruffle

Ruffle

Sepal

The many ruffles of the
petunia should be shaded
in values 5 and 6.

1

2

4

3

Petunia

Petunias, which adapt readily to most areas and bloom prolifically, are widely used in parks and gardens. Petunias come in many varieties, colors, and sizes; the flowers can be single-petaled, double-petaled, or ruffled.

Flower Shape

A tube-shaped flower with a flared mouth.

Color

A variety of shades of rose, blue, purple, dark reddish violet, yellow, and white.

Order of Hooking

Center. The center is yellow.

Petals. Begin hooking the flared area above the center of the flower. Use value 6 above the curved line and around the yellow center. Hook four fingers in value 6 with an end-loop-loop-end; the fingers follow the "veins" on the illustration in fanlike curves. Following the curves of the fingers, shade out to a lighter value, hooking at least two loops at the end of each curved finger. Shade the ruffles along the inner curves with darker values.

To hook the flared area below the center, reverse the shading by hooking the lightest value below the curved line and shading out to darker values at the lower edge of the flower. Hook the sepals in medium values of green before you hook the tube. Complete the flower by hooking the tube in value 2 on the outer edges and in value 1 in the middle of the tube.

Leaves. The petunia leaf is simple in shape. Choose a yellow-green or a true green. Try hooking the veins in the color of another flower.

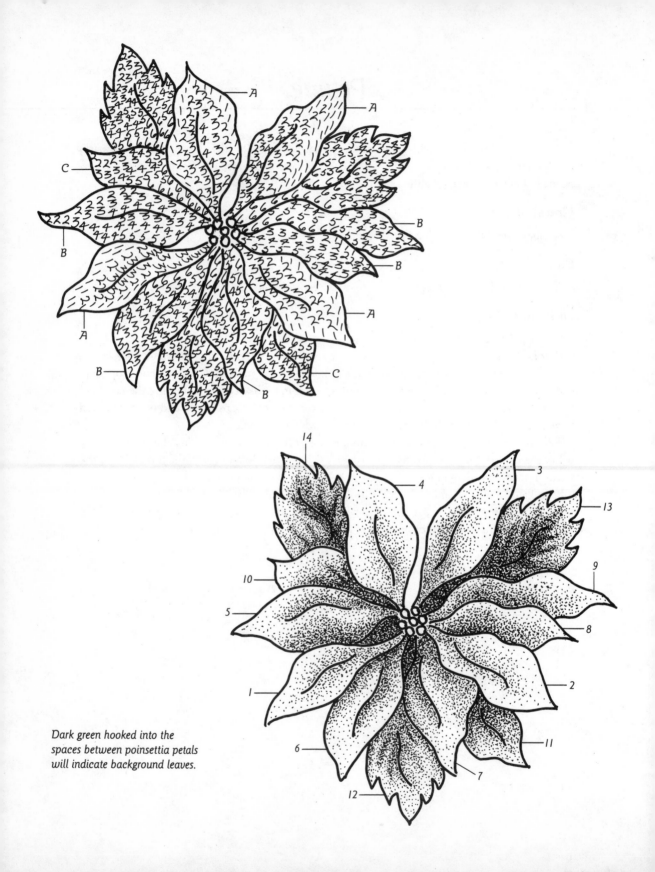

Dark green hooked into the
spaces between poinsettia petals
will indicate background leaves.

Poinsettia

The poinsettia is a beautiful plant that is widely grown for the Christmas season. The tiny yellow-green flowers are in the center of the poinsettia. The showy feature of the plant is the bright red petallike bracts, especially in contrast to the deep green leaves.

Flower Shape

There are many narrow bracts.

Color

Red, pink, and white.

Order of Hooking

Center. Hook the center in yellow-green spot dye. Pull the loops slightly higher than usual.

Petals. Although the poinsettia bracts are not really petals, for convenience they will be referred to as A, B, and C petals. Begin by hooking the vein in each petal in brown or brown spot dye. Hook the four A petals in values 4, 3, 2, and 1. Hook value 4 or 3 along both sides of the vein, shading out to value 1 along the outer edges. Hook one half of the petal, then the other half.

Hook the five B petals dark at the center base and where the petal goes under another petal. Shade from value 6 or 5 to value 2 or 1.

The C petals will be the darkest petals. Use value 6 at the center base and where the petals go under other petals, shading out with values 5, 4, and 3, or even 2.

Note the small open areas between some of the petals. Hook them in dark green to give the impression that there are green leaves behind the flower. If you hook them in the background color of your rug, you may create a "bull's-eye" effect.

Leaves. Choose a true green for the poinsettia leaf. Hook the veins in brown spot dye, or use a value from your flower color. Follow the illustrations to determine the placement of color.

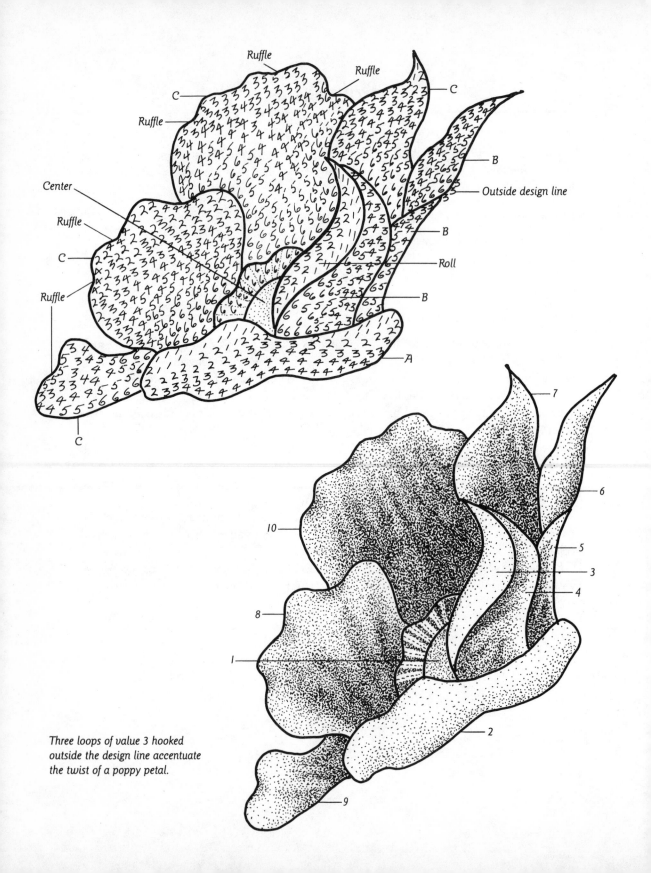

Ruffle *Ruffle*

C *C*

Ruffle *B*

Center *Outside design line*

Ruffle

C *B*

Ruffle *Roll*

B

C *A*

7

10

6

5
8 3
4

1

2

9

*Three loops of value 3 hooked
outside the design line accentuate
the twist of a poppy petal.*

Poppy

The splendid poppies that bloom in our gardens derive from the oriental poppy indigenous to western Asia.

Flower Shape

An open-petaled flower with large petals.

Color

Red, orange, pink, lavender, and mahogany.

Order of Hooking

Center. Using either a strip of black and another of white, or a black-and-white check, hook the small circular area first, then the lines radiating from the center.

Petals. The light-colored A petal curls upward from the bottom. Hook value 4 along the bottom edge, doing only the middle portion, not the entire length of the petal. Hook two rows that extend two loops beyond the first row. Then hook a bulge at the inner curve on the bottom. Hook value 3 with a bulge at the small inner curve on the left bottom edge. Follow with nicely curved rows of value 2, and fill in with value 1.

Hook the roll of the first B petal with value 3 along the outer edge, shading inward to value 1. Hook the rest of the petal with value 6 at the center base and where the petal goes under the roll. Hook two fingers in value 6 with an end-loop-loop-end. Follow the fingers, shading out to value 3.

The second B petal is long, narrow, and twisted. Begin at the bottom, shading from value 6 at the center base and where it goes under the other B petal to value 3 at the top edge. Extend value 3 three loops beyond the top edge to make the petal twist. Shade the upper part of the petal from value 6 on the right side to value 3 on the left. The left side of the petal must be at least two values lighter than the petal next to it.

Hook the pointed C petal with value 6 at the center base and where it goes under the B petals. Hook two fingers of value 6 with an end-loop-loop-end. Shade out to value 2 or 1, following the fingers.

Hook the second C petal with two rows of value 6 at the center base and four fingers with an end-loop-loop-end. Shade out to value 2, repeating a value if necessary. Shade the ruffles with value 4; follow the illustrations to determine the color placement.

Shade the smallest C petal from value 6 to value 3 with no fingers.

Hook the largest and darkest C petal with the technique of feathering described in Chapter 2. Hook value 6 at the center base and where the petal goes under other petals. Begin feathering with value 6, shading out to value 3. Remember to shade the ruffles.

Leaves. Hook the poppy's large, feathery leaves in a yellow-green.

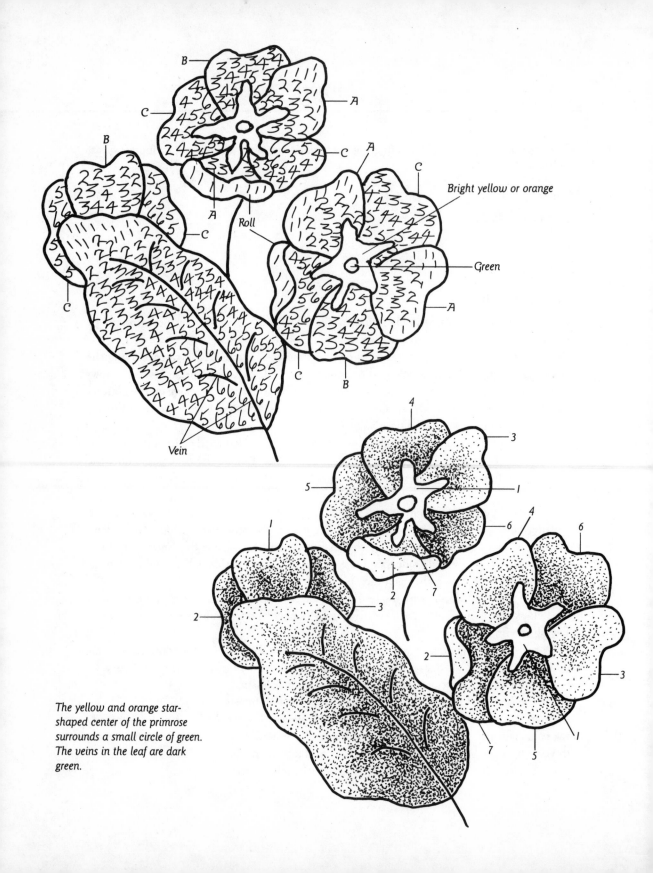

The yellow and orange star-shaped center of the primrose surrounds a small circle of green. The veins in the leaf are dark green.

Primrose

The primrose has an old-fashioned charm. The most familiar primrose, the polyantha, grows from eight to ten inches tall and bears immense clusters of single or double flowers in spring. The majority of species favor moist, peaty soil in a cool, shady spot.

Flower Shape

An open-petaled flower with small petals.

Color

Yellow (most common color), pink, blue, red, mauve, and white.

Order of Hooking

Center. Hook the small circle in the middle of the center with a medium light green. Hook the star shape with strips of bright yellow and orange.

Petals. Hook the flower on the right first. The flower has two A petals, two B petals, and one C petal. Hook the roll in value 1. Since the petals are small, you will mostly use only three values. Make sure the edges of the A petals are light enough to contrast with the shadow hooked on the next petal.

The flower at the top has two A petals, one B petal, and two C petals. The flower on the left has one B petal and two dark C petals. Follow the illustrations carefully as you work.

Leaves. The leaves of the primrose are yellow-green. Use a different swatch to make the veins dark green. Follow the illustrations to determine the placement of color. Hook half of the leaf at a time.

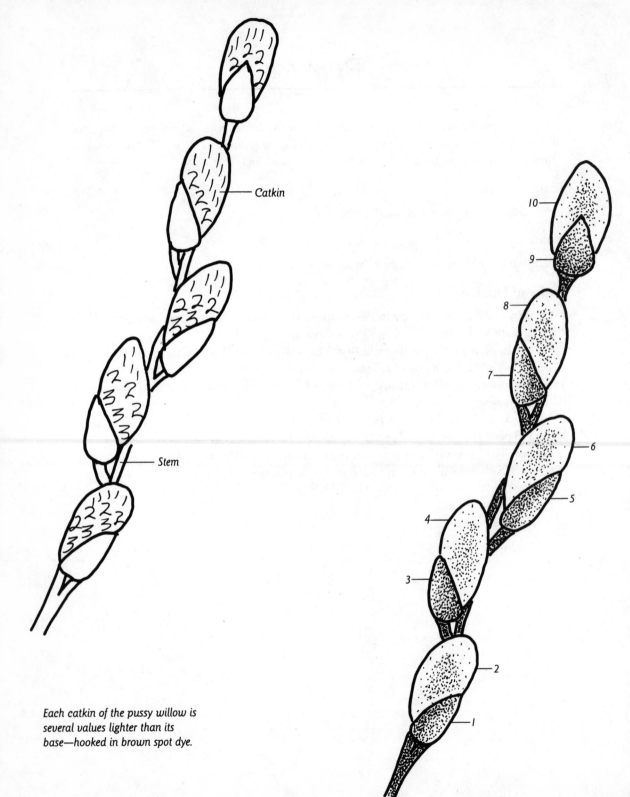

Catkin

Stem

Each catkin of the pussy willow is several values lighter than its base—hooked in brown spot dye.

Pussy Willow

Even as the cold blasts of winter continue, the pussy willow sends forth fuzzy catkins as a gentle reminder that spring is coming. Long twigs of pussy willow that are cut and added to flower arrangements will often root in water. Then they can be planted outside to produce new trees.

Color

Use a light brown swatch and complement it with a dark brown spot dye.

Order of Hooking

Catkins and Stem. Hook the stem in a dark brown. Hook the base of each catkin with a brown spot dye; follow the contour of the base as you hook. Use light values to hook the catkins. Hook the lower three catkins in values 3, 2, and 1 and the upper two in values 2 and 1.

If you plan to use your project as a wall hanging, try using sheep's wool to hook the catkins. Pull the loops up about half an inch. Then clip the loops with scissors to shape the catkins, cutting the wool lower at the edges of the catkins and a little higher at their centers. This will create a wonderful three-dimensional effect. Try to find a creamy white sheep's wool. If your wool is too white, dye part of it in silver-gray, then mix the two together before hooking.

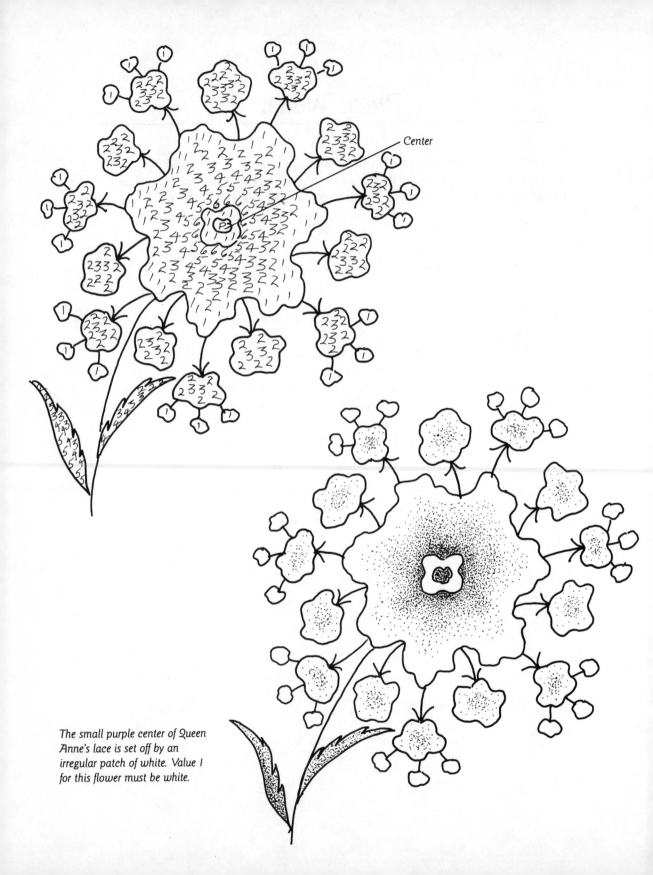

Center

The small purple center of Queen Anne's lace is set off by an irregular patch of white. Value 1 for this flower must be white.

Queen Anne's Lace

This weed is a member of the carrot family and thrives in cultivated fields, meadows, along the roadside, and even in our gardens. The flat-topped, lacy, white flower clusters have a single dark purple flower in the center. This pretty weed flowers from June to September. Stem, leaves, and root have the familiar carrot odor.

Flower Shape

Irregular.

Color

White to gray or white to gray-green.

Order of Hooking

Center. The flower is made up of small clusters similar to snowflakes. Hook an end-loop-end of purple in the center of the main cluster. Follow the illustrations for placement of colors, noting that this is a white flower.

Leaves. These are finely divided and look like parsely. Hook in a true green or a yellow-green. The stems joining the clusters will be hooked in a medium to light green.

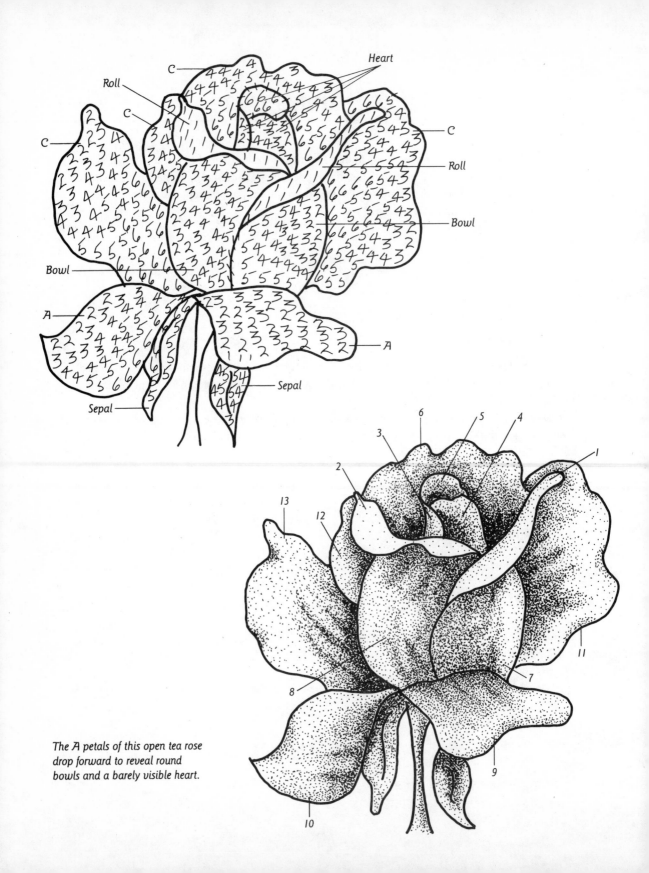

The A petals of this open tea rose
drop forward to reveal round
bowls and a barely visible heart.

Rose

The rose is the queen of all flowers. There is constant reference to the beauty, the color, or the fragrance of roses in art, history, literature, and contemporary advertising. Centuries of careful cultivation and cross-breeding have created almost thirteen thousand identifiable varieties of roses. Roses are as varied as the countries in which they originate. There are massive blooms the size of saucers and miniature roses that will slip through a wedding ring. There are climbers, ramblers, shrubs, and trees. The most familiar and popular rose is the hybrid tea rose, which accounts for virtually all of the cut roses sold by florists.

Flower Shape

An open-petaled flower.

Color

All the shades from white through pink, yellow, red, and maroon.

Order of Hooking

Flowers. To hook an open rose, identify the four parts of the rose and hook them in order. Hook the roll or rolls in the lightest value. Then hook the heart, the dark, tightly rolled petals at the center of the rose. Then hook the bowl (there are usually two bowls) in medium values. And finally, hook the A, B, and C petals.

Open tea rose. This rose is an open-petaled, "cup-and-saucer" flower. Hook the two rolls in value 1. As you hook the roll on the right, extend value 1 along the line that divides the two bowls of the rose.

Next hook the three parts that make up the heart of the rose, following the illustrations carefully as you work. Then hook the two bowls, noting that one bowl overlaps the other.

Finally, hook the petals. Since the petals are large, you will need to hook fingers to shade them. Hook the two sepals at the base of the rose in green.

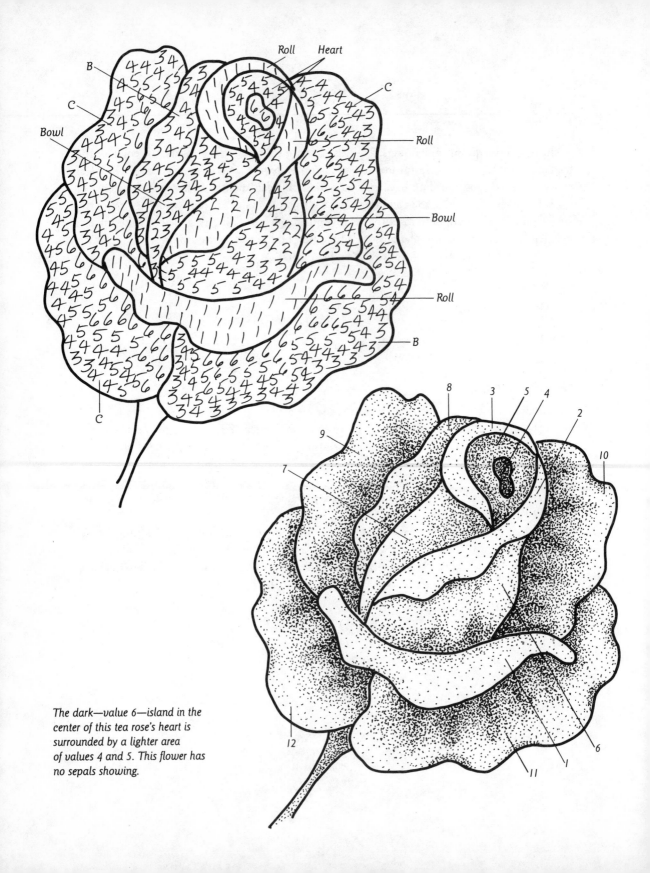

The dark—value 6—island in the center of this tea rose's heart is surrounded by a lighter area of values 4 and 5. This flower has no sepals showing.

Rose

Tea rose. This rose is also an open-petaled, cup-and-saucer flower. Hook the three rolls first. When you hook the diagonal roll in values 2 and 1, extend value 1 down along the vertical line that meets the bottom roll.

The heart of the rose is made up of two parts surrounded by the circular roll. Hook the small island in the heart with value 6 and the area around it with values 4 and 5.

Hook the two bowls on either side of the diagonal roll, shading where the bowls go under the rolls with value 5.

Then hook the four large petals, making them dark at the center base and where they go under other petals. Since these petals have broad bases, begin hooking them in value 6 regardless of their positions. Follow the illustrations carefully to determine the placement of the fingers and the details of shading.

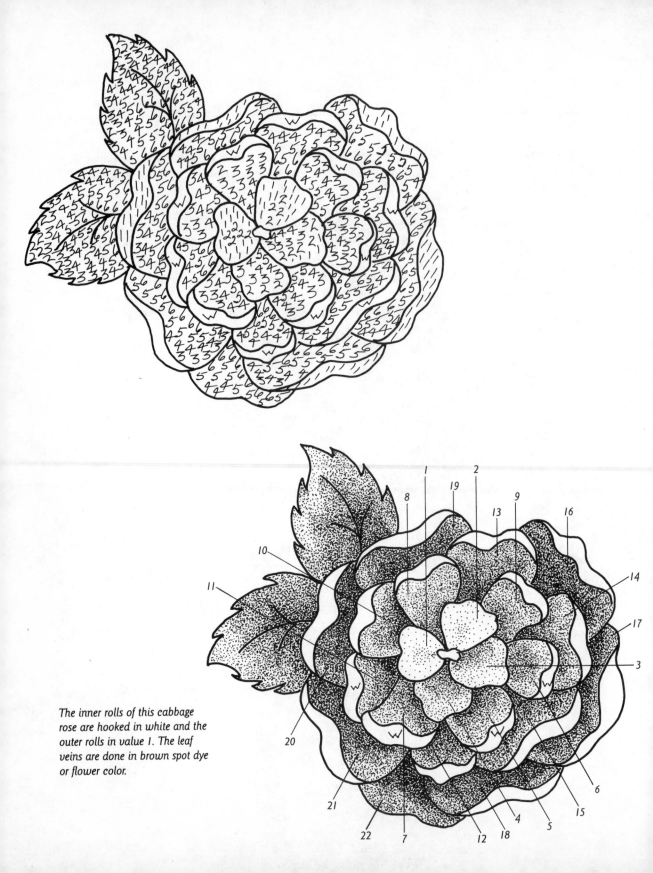

The inner rolls of this cabbage rose are hooked in white and the outer rolls in value 1. The leaf veins are done in brown spot dye or flower color.

Rose

Cabbage rose. This rose is a many-petaled open flower. A cabbage rose is usually very large; it may have as many as a hundred overlapping petals—like a cabbage.

Hook the center in a yellow-gold. Then hook the petals around the center first, working out to the petals at the outer edge of the flower. The petals near the center will be the lightest; the under petals have rolls on the edges that will be hooked in white or value 1. The petals themselves will become darker as they near the edge of the flower. As you work, watch the petals around the one you are hooking to provide the correct contrast. Follow the illustrations carefully.

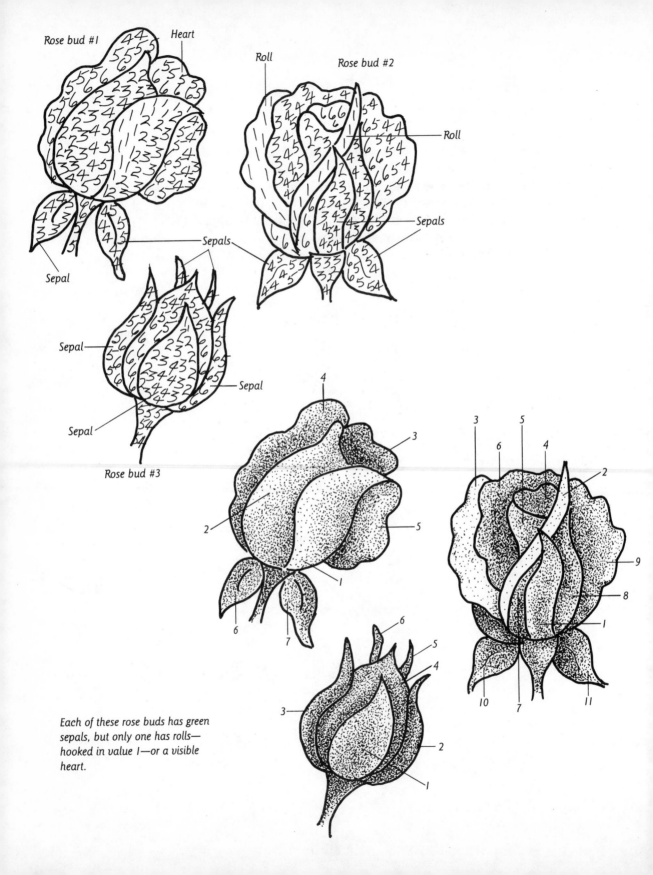

Rose bud #1

Heart

Roll

Rose bud #2

Roll

Sepals

Sepal

Sepal

Sepals

Sepal

Sepal

Sepal

Rose bud #3

4

3

2

5

1

6

7

6

5

4

3

2

1

3

6

5

4

2

9

8

1

10

7

11

Each of these rose buds has green sepals, but only one has rolls—hooked in value 1—or a visible heart.

Rose

Rose bud #1. This is a lovely rose bud with a wraparound bowl, another bowl, and three petals. Follow the illustrations to create a delightful flower.

Rose bud #2. This rose bud has three sepals, two at the base and one up in front of the petals. Hook the front sepal first, using a green. Then hook the diagonal roll and the roll on the left in value 1.

Complete the two parts of the heart of the rose bud before hooking the bowl, which is divided by the green sepal. Hook the bowl in dark and medium values. Follow the illustrations to determine the placement of color on the petals.

Rose bud #3. This is a tight bud with green sepals enclosing the compact rose petals. Hook the sepals first, using a green. Then hook the rose bud in dark values.

Leaves. The rose leaf is medium sized with a toothed edge. Use a true green or a yellow-green for the leaves and a brown spot dye or a flower color for the veins.

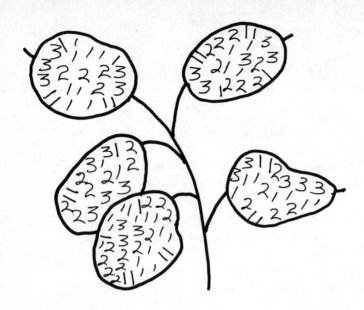

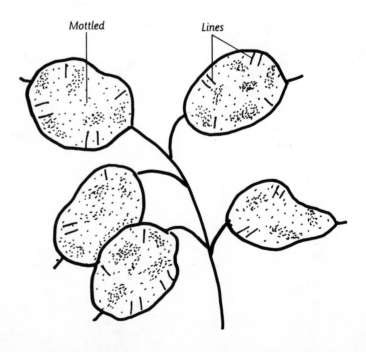

Mottled

Lines

The mottled appearance of these
silver dollars is created with a
mixture of values 1, 2, and 3 of a
white swatch. A brown swatch—
value 5 for stems and 6 for lines
and outlines—holds the silver dollars together.

Silver Dollar

The silver dollar, sometimes called "honesty," is a biennial plant with odorless flowers that develop into large, flat seed pods. When the outer covering of the seed pods is rubbed off and the seeds fall, a mother-of-pearl coin is revealed. Silver dollars add much to winter arrangements of dried flowers.

Shape

The silver dollar is irregularly shaped.

Color

Woody brown with marbled "coins" in white swatch.

Order of Hooking

Silver Dollars. Hook the stem, the outline of each silver dollar, and the sets of lines just inside the outline with dark values of a light-brown swatch. To hook the silver dollar, use the three lightest values of a white swatch, mixing them as you hook to obtain a mottled effect.

You can create a wonderful look by using sheep's wool for the silver dollars. As you work, change the tension of your hooking; the wool will look darker when you hook the loops close together and it will look lighter when you hook them farther apart. If you plan to use your hooked piece as a wall hanging, you can produce a stunning visual effect by cutting the tops of the loops with a pair of bent hooking scissors. This will make the silver dollars look flat and it will also recreate their typical shiny luster.

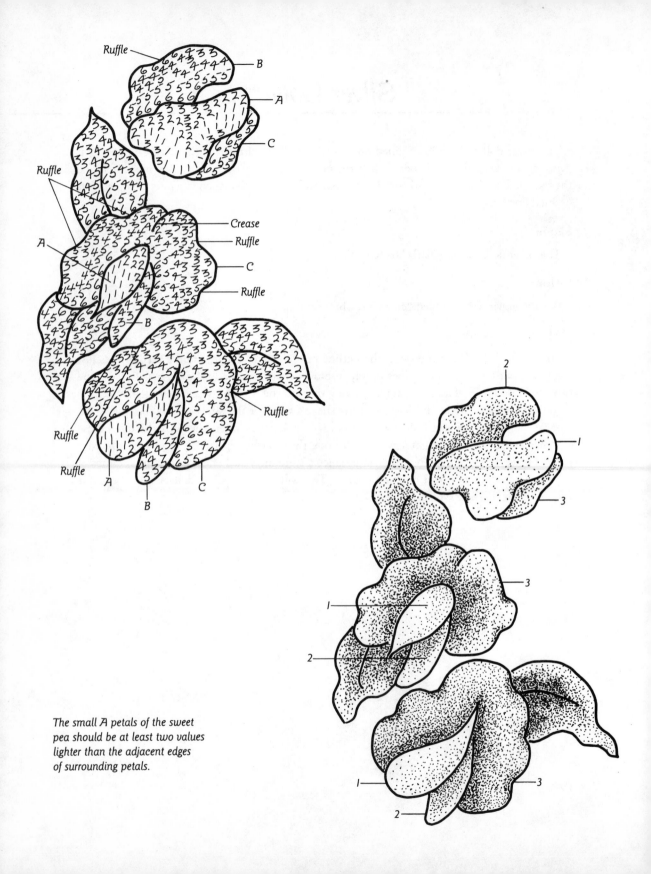

The small A petals of the sweet pea should be at least two values lighter than the adjacent edges of surrounding petals.

Sweet Pea

The sweet pea was popular in Edwardian England after it was introduced from its native Sicily. Its fragrant blossoms resemble little sunbonnets. Sweet peas make lovely cut flowers that brighten any room.

Flower Shape

An irregularly shaped flower.

Color

White, cream, pink, salmon, scarlet, mauve, or blue.

Order of Hooking

Flowers. Hook the flower at the bottom of the group first. Use values 2 and 1 to hook the teardrop-shaped A petal. Hook the teardrop B petal next to it in values 4 and 3. To hook the large C petal, use value 6 where the petal goes under the teardrop petals, shading out to value 3. Shade the inner curves of the ruffles by hooking an end-loop-end or an end-loop-loop-end of value 5.

Hook the flower in the middle of the group the same way you hooked the first flower—with one exception. Notice the crease at the top of the C petal. Hook the area to the right of the crease two values lighter than the area to the left of the crease. Follow the illustrations carefully as you work.

To hook the flower at the top of the group, hook the A petal in values 3, 2, and 1. Hook the larger B petal in darker values and the small B petal in the darkest values 6 and 5.

Leaves. The sweet pea has small, simple leaves. Hook the leaves with a yellow-green swatch and the veins with a brown spot dye.

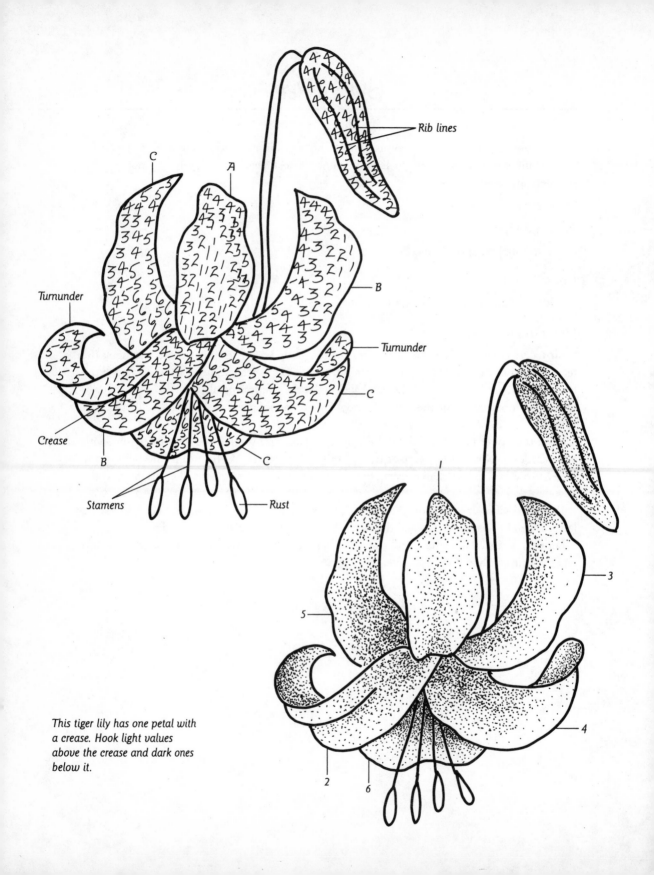

Rib lines

C

A

Turnunder

Crease

B

Stamens

Rust

B

Turnunder

C

C

This tiger lily has one petal with
a crease. Hook light values
above the crease and dark ones
below it.

1

3

5

4

2

6

Tiger Lily

The tiger lily belongs to one of the largest families of flowering plants. They grow three to four feet tall and have large orange-red flowers with purple or reddish brown dots.

Flower Shape

A large bell-shaped flower.

Color

Fiery gold or orange-red.

Order of Hooking

Center. The stamens are green with rust-colored pods.

Petals. Hook the base of the A petal with value 2, highlighting with value 1, and shading out to value 4.

Hook the turnunder of the first B petal with value 5 along the outer curve, shading to value 3 on the inner curve. Hook the petal with value 5 at the center base, shading to value 4. Before you complete this petal, hook the crease with an end-loop-loop-end of value 1 above it and another of value 3 below it. Finish shading the petal from the base with values 3, 2, and 1, contrasting it with adjacent petals.

Hook the second B petal with value 5 at the center base and halfway up the inner curve. Follow along this curve with value 4, extending it three loops beyond value 5. Add a finger of value 4 with an end-loop-loop-end near the petal's base. Then shade out with values 3, 2, and 1, following the finger of value 4.

Hook the turnunder on the first C petal in values 5 and 4. Hook the C petal with value 6 at the center base and where it goes under the B petal. Hook in value 5, extending it beyond value 6, and add a finger of value 5 with an end-loop-loop-end. Shade out with values 4, 3, 2, and 1, following the finger of value 5.

Hook the second C petal with value 6 at the center base and where it goes under the A petal. Hook a finger in value 6 with an end-loop-loop-end. Follow this with values 5, 4, and 3, but darken the tip with values 4 and 5.

Hook the third C petal with value 6 at its center base and where it goes under the other petals. Shade with value 5, working around the stamens.

Complete the flower by hooking end-loop-end dots in purple on all the petals.

Hook the two lines of the bud in values 6 and 5. Hook the base in value 4, extending it toward the tip, along the edges and between the lines. Shade with values 3 and 2.

Leaves. The tiger lily has many narrow leaves. Hook them with mock shading in a true green or a yellow-green.

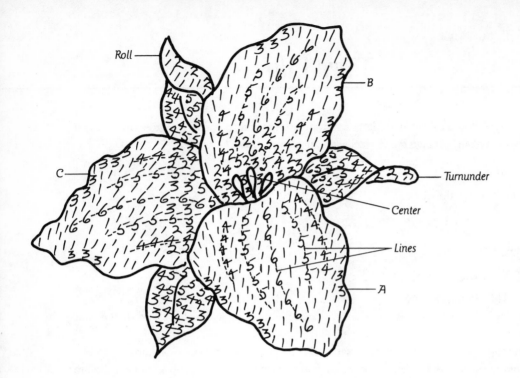

Roll

B

C

Turnunder

Center

Lines

A

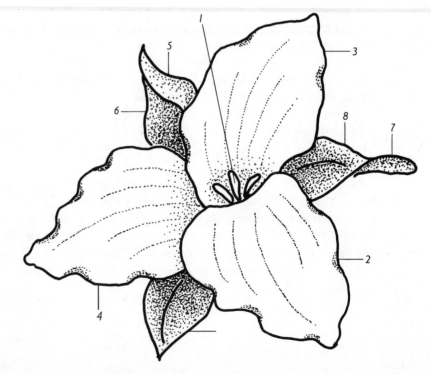

5

6

1

3

8

7

2

4

The petals of this trillium are
hooked along the contour of their
gently curving lines.

Trillium

The trillium is a lovely wild flower that grows in wooded areas, but it can also be cultivated in a shaded garden with minimal care. As its name might imply, the trillium has three petals, three sepals, and three leaflets.

Flower Shape

An open-petaled flower with large petals.

Color

White.

Order of Hooking

Center. Hook the center in yellow-green.

Petals. The A petal has five curved lines. Begin by hooking the center line in value 6. Then hook the two curved lines on either side of the center line in value 5, and finally, hook the outer lines in value 4. Shade the ruffles with an end-loop-end in value 3 along the inner curves of the petal. Then fill in the rest of the petal with value 1, following the contour of the curved lines.

To hook the B petal, hook the curved lines as you did on the A petal. Hook the ruffles in value 3. Then hook around the stamens with value 3. Hook an end-loop-loop-end of value 2 between the curved lines, filling in with value 1.

Hook the curved lines in the C petal as you did before. Hook the ruffles in value 3. Since this petal is darker than the others, hook values 5 and 4 near the base of the petal, shading to values 3 and 2 before finishing the petal in value 1. Although different values are used in this flower, the swatch is so light that the flower will appear white.

To hook the first sepal, hook the roll in value 2 and 1. Then hook the vein in a brown spot dye. Use value 5 at the base of the sepal, adding values 4 and 3 if there is room.

Hook the turnunder on the second sepal with value 2 on the outer curve and value 1 on the inner curve. Use value 6 at the base of the sepal, completing it with values 5 and 4.

To hook the third sepal, hook the vein in brown spot dye. Then hook the base in value 5, shading out to values 4 and 3.

Leaves. Hook the trillium leaves in yellow-green.

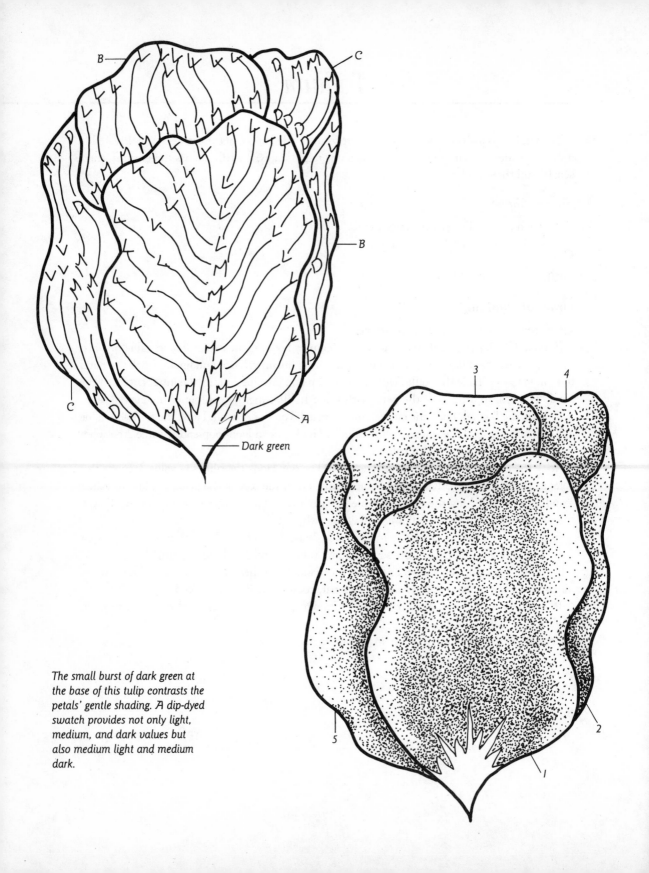

— Dark green

The small burst of dark green at the base of this tulip contrasts the petals' gentle shading. A dip-dyed swatch provides not only light, medium, and dark values but also medium light and medium dark.

Tulip

In Holland, the production of tulip bulbs is a major industry. The tulip's name is derived from an ancient Persian word for turban, *taliban*, since the tulip flower is shaped like an inverted turban.

Flower Shape

An open-petaled flower with large petals.

Color

White, yellow, red, pink, and bluish black.

Dip-dyed wool is ideal for hooking tulips. You can dip-dye swatches that range from dark red through bright red to pink, from dark red through orange-red to yellow, or from purple through mauve to yellow. (See Chapter 4 for directions.) You will appreciate the results you get with a minimum of effort.

Order of Hooking

Petals. Study the illustrations carefully. Three different tulips are shown. Each one is marked to indicate the shade of dip dye to be used: D (dark), M (medium), and L (light). As you work with the dip-dyed colors, have fun and experiment!

Hook the dip-dyed strip from the base of the petal to the tip. If the petal is large, you will be able to use the entire strip. But if the petal is small and if you want to include all the shades, pull up a high loop to get the shade you want. You may have to pull up several high loops. Cut the high loops off, but don't discard them; you may need them somewhere else in the flower.

To hook a petal that is mostly dark, cut the dark end off a strip of dip-dyed wool. Hook the dark end in, and then continue hooking with the dark end of a full strip. This will give you enough dark color, as well as the lighter shades you need.

If there are small areas in the petal that you want to hook entirely in dark, medium, or light shades, cut the required shade from the dip-dyed strips. Save the rest of each strip to use somewhere else in the flower.

As you hook with dip-dyed strips, follow the contour of the petal. Don't hook straight rows on a rounded petal. Follow the illustrations carefully as you work.

Leaves. The tulip has long, narrow "strap" leaves. The leaves may be straight or twisted, or they may have turnunders. Dip-dyed strips work well for this kind of leaf.

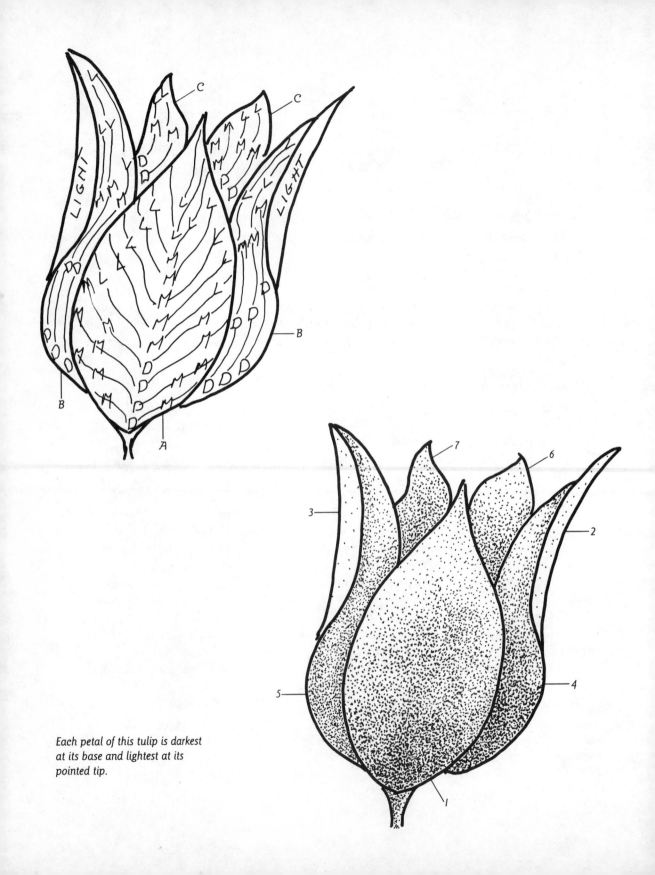

Each petal of this tulip is darkest
at its base and lightest at its
pointed tip.

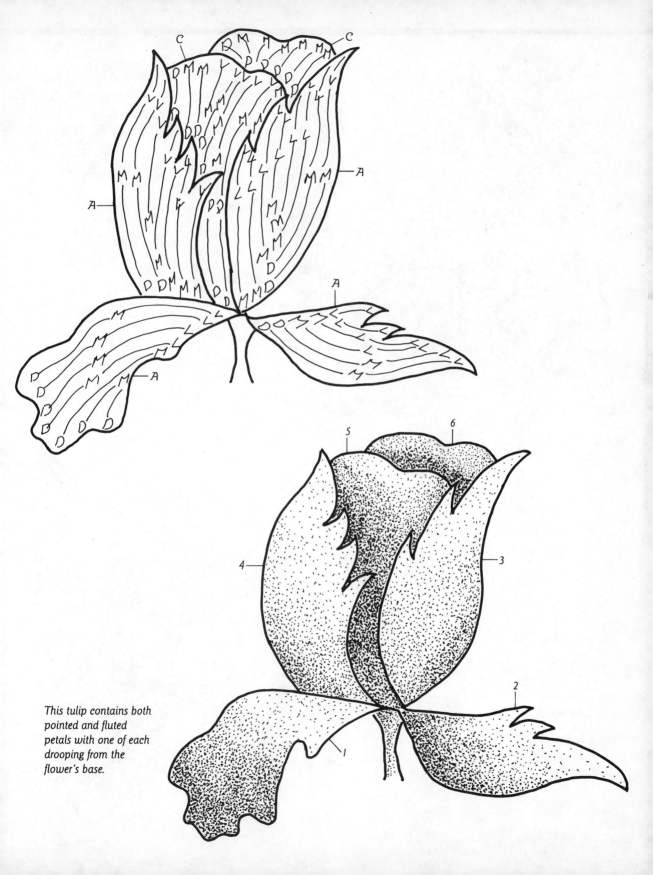

This tulip contains both pointed and fluted petals with one of each drooping from the flower's base.

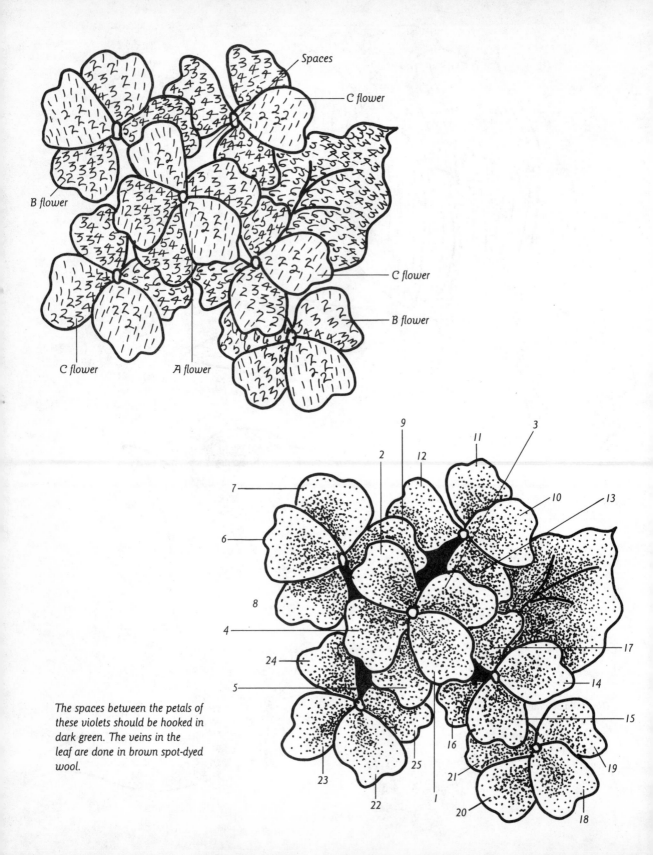

Spaces

C flower

B flower

C flower

C flower

A flower

B flower

The spaces between the petals of
these violets should be hooked in
dark green. The veins in the
leaf are done in brown spot-dyed
wool.

Violet

There are more than three hundred species of violets in the world; eighty species are found in North America. For centuries, violets have been a symbol of humility in works of art and literature. The violet, with its attractive five-petaled flowers and heart-shaped leaves, was a favorite flower in the festivals of Rome.

Flower Shape

An open-petaled flower with small leaves.

Color

Deep purple, lavender, red, pink, yellow, and white.

You can hook the group of violets with one swatch or two swatches. If you use one swatch, you must make the violets at the top of the group light, so that the violets below will stand out. If you use two swatches, each violet will be better defined. Some effective two-color combinations are lavender and red-purple, red-purple and pink, or white and lavender.

Order of Hooking

Center. The tiny centers are yellow or gold. Try to keep them tidy by hooking an end-loop-end: pull up an end, hook a loop, then pull the end up in the same hole that the first end was pulled through.

Petals. Hook the violets at the top of the group first. Hook all the A petals in values 1 and 2. Keep the B petals as light as possible, so that the C petals can be distinguished from them. Hook the spaces that are visible behind the group of violets in a dark green.

Leaves. Hook the violet's heart-shaped leaves in a true green or in a blue-green or yellow-green. Hook the veins in a brown spot-dyed wool or in the color of another flower. Follow the illustrations carefully as you work.

Helpful Hints

Pin a small magnet on your burlap pattern to hold your hook and scissors when you aren't using them.

Protect a light-colored background by placing a piece of plastic wrap over your pattern and under your hoop. Cut a 5-inch hole in the plastic to work through. You can move the plastic wrap as you work on various sections of your pattern. This really keeps your work clean.

Cut your wool into strips 10 to 18 inches long.

Try using dark blue or navy blue wool overdyed with Turkey Red dye for a good plum-colored background.

Try using aqua wool overdyed with Orange dye for a good dark brown.

Distinguish real wool from synthetic fabric by rubbing a piece against your cheek. If it feels scratchy, it's probably a synthetic fabric. If it feels soft, it's a wool. You may also try holding a lit match to a small strand of the fabric. If it flares, it's synthetic. If it smells like burning hair, it's wool.

Create a more detailed separation in a many-petaled flower by hooking a darker color between several of the petals.

Estimate the amount of wool needed for a background to be four times the area of the background for strips of a #3 or #4 cut, five times the area for wider strips.

Expect a 3½-by-9-inch swatch to hook any one of the following:
• two 3½- to 4-inch flowers plus one bud
• eight small leaves
• two large leaves plus one small leaf
• four medium leaves plus one small leaf
• five small flowers plus three buds

Watch the middle values when hooking with a swatch. You tend to run out of these unless you apportion the values of the swatch carefully.

Do not consider just the color when purchasing a swatch. Examine the gradation of the whole swatch: you want a smooth transition from value to value.

Do not reject a swatch just because it is somewhat mottled. Evenly dyed swatches are very nice, but great effects can be created with mottled wools.

Sources of Supplies

APPLETON KRAFTS & SUPPLIES, 50 Appleton Ave., South Hamilton, MA 01982. Complete line of rug-hooking supplies.

BRAID-AID, 466 Washington St., Pembroke, MA 02359. Complete line of supplies for hooked and braided rugs.

THE BURLAP ROOM, 46 Little Lake Dr., Barrie, Ontario, Canada L4M 4Y8. Complete line of rug-hooking supplies.

DESIGNS TO DREAM ON, Jane McGown Flynn, Inc., P.O. Box 1301, Sterling, MA 01564. Complete line of rug-hooking supplies. Catalog available.

DiFRANZA DESIGNS, 25 Bow St., North Reading, MA 01864. Patterns and kits for rugs. Complete line of rug-hooking supplies. Catalog available.

DORR MILL STORE, P.O. Box 88, Guild, NH 03754-0088. Wool by the yard. Catalog available.

FORESTHEART STUDIO, 21 South Carroll St., Frederick, MD 21701. Rug hooking, weaving, spinning, and other uncommon fiber arts. Supplies, equipment, instruction, and finished work.

HEIRLOOM CARE, INC., P.O. Box 2540, Westwood, MA 02090. Rug cleaner for the professional care of hooked rugs. Includes natural-fiber brush and complete instructions.

JACQUELINE DESIGNS, 237 Pine Point Rd., Scarborough, ME 04074. Complete line of supplies for hooked rugs. Catalog available.

MAYFLOWER TEXTILE COMPANY, P.O. Box 329, Franklin, MA 02038. Manufacturers of the Puritan Lap Frame.

JOAN MOSHIMER (W. Cushing and Company), P.O. Box 351, North St., Kennebunkport, ME 04046. Cushing's Perfection Dyes, patterns, instructions, kits, a complete line of supplies, and finished rugs.

JANE OLSON, P.O. Box 351, Hawthorne, CA 90250. Complete line of supplies for rug hooking and braiding. Catalog available.

PRO CHEMICAL & DYE, INC., P.O. Box 14, Somerset, MA 02726. Commercial dyes, pigments, and auxiliaries for the surface coloration of fiber. Catalog available.

RAGS TO RUGS CRAFT SHOPPE, 14 Eastmoor Dr., Truro, Nova Scotia, Canada B2N 2X3. Complete line of rug-hooking supplies.

RITTERMERE-HURST-FIELD, 45 Tyler St., Box 487, Aurora, Ontario, Canada L4G 3L6. Complete line of rug-hooking supplies.

RUG HOOKING Magazine, Cameron and Kelker Sts., P.O. Box 15760, Harrisburg, PA 17105. Bimonthly source of information on traditional hand-hooked rugs. Provides how-to's, historical profiles, dye formulas, and patterns. $19.95 for one year's subscription ($24.95 in Canada, $35.00 overseas).

RUTH ANN'S WOOL, R.D. #4, Box 340, Muncy, PA 17756. Wool in natural, white, and 28 colors.

SEA HOLLY HOOKED RUGS, Sea Holly Square, 1906 N. Bayview Dr., Kill Devil Hills, NC 27948. Hand-dyed wool by the yard or pound. Finished pieces and rug-hooking supplies also available.

SWEET BRIAR STUDIO, 866 Main St., Hope Valley, RI 02832. Patterns and supplies for rug hooking. Catalog available.

THE TRIPLE OVER DYE FAMILY, 187 Jane Dr., Syracuse, NY 13219. How-to booklets with formulas for triple overdyeing.